KNOW
WHAT
YOU
BELIEVE

Paul E. Little

VICTOR BOOKS
a division of SP Publications, Inc., Wheaton, Illinois
Offices also in Fullerton, California • Whitby, Ontario, Canada • London, England

Fourteenth printing, 1979

Printed in the United States of America
Library of Congress Catalog Card No. 76-105667

ISBN-0-88207-024-X

VICTOR BOOKS
A division of SP Publications, Inc.
P.O. Box 1825 • Wheaton, Ill. 60187

Contents

A Letter to You!

Dear Reader·

Precisely what do you believe about the deity of Jesus Christ? About the Atonement? What would you say if someone asked you why you are sure that the Holy Spirit is a Person rather than merely an influence? What do you believe about God? About the Bible? About Satan? The angels?

Most of us — even if we once took a course in doctrine — tend to be a bit rusty in our theology. We could stand a refresher course in this subject! And especially is this true in a generation apparently dedicated to abolishing "absolutes" and that resists the very notion that truth is propositional — that we can communicate it to other people in simple sentences.

The amount of loose thinking abroad today is staggering. As people in general pay less and less attention to "religion," and as even Christians pay less and less attention to the Bible, the result is that "the faith once for all delivered to the saints" is positively imperiled by the ignorance of those responsible to defend and perpetuate it.

This volume is eminently timely. It will bring to the minds of evangelical adults truths they may have lost sight of or perhaps never knew. New converts will enjoy having at their fingertips a brief treatment of Christian doctrine for easy reference. Young Christians will find their spiritual maturity hastened by the easily assimilated truths here presented. And those who have made no commitment to Christ will find powerful motivation for such action in these pages.

Before you plunge ahead, a word of caution may be in order. Though Mr. Little has done a masterful job in presenting theological truth on a level where "average" adults can assimilate it, remember that some of his subjects are ultimately profound. You may find yourself challenged by chapters 2, 5, 7, or 8, for instance, but don't abandon the book or conclude that you simply cannot manage it. Read the passage over, or return to it later, or discuss it with your pastor. You'll find that the more you need to study a chapter, the more significant it will become to you.

Good *reading*, then! And good *studying!* You will be spiritually richer for having mastered the contents of this book!

The Editors

Acknowledgments

The publishers acknowledge with thanks permission to use materials from various sources, including such standard reference works as the *New Bible Dictionary* and the *International Standard Bible Encyclopedia* (published by Eerdmans Publishing Co., Grand Rapids) and the publications of Moody Press, Chicago. Material is also used from these publications of Inter-Varsity Fellowship, London: *Ministers of God,* © 1964; *The Death of Christ,* © 1951; *Evangelism and the Sovereignty of God,* © 1961; and *In Understanding Be Men,* © 1936. These four books are available from your Christian bookseller or Inter-Varsity Press, Box F, Downers Grove, Illinois 60515.

Chapter 1

The Bible

What is the Bible — this Book that has far and away been the best seller of all history and has been translated into more languages than any other book?

"Bible" means "book." But what kind of book is the Bible? Some suggest it is a record of man's religious striving toward and encounters with God — an essentially human book. Until the latter half of the last century, however, the historic Christian Church had always seen the Bible as far more than this — namely, as the written Word of God. There was no doctrine on which there was greater unity among Christians. Not until recently have widespread doubts been raised.

The question of the Bible is a crucial one because it involves the whole issue of revelation. How can we know God exists? How can we know about Him, even if He *does* exist? It is clear that our finite minds cannot penetrate His infinity. Job asked, "Canst thou by searching find out God?" (Job 11:7) The answer is, Only as God takes the initiative in revealing Himself.

God has revealed Himself in several ways. Nature and creation are proof that God exists and that He is powerful (Rom. 1:19, 20). God has revealed Himself through history, particularly in His dealings with Israel and the nations surrounding her. Such Old Testament expressions as, "Then Manasseh knew that the Lord He was God" (2 Chron. 33:13), reflect recognition of God because of His activity in the affairs of men and nations.

God's revelation came to man not only through events themselves, but through the words of the prophets who *interpreted* the events. "The Word of the Lord came to me" and, "thus saith the Lord," are recurring phrases throughout the Old Testament (cf. Ezek. 7:1; 12:1; Zech. 8:1; Ex. 4:22; 1 Sam. 2:27) of what is called propositional revelation.

God's fullest revelation came in the person of His Son, Jesus Christ. The writer to the Hebrews summarizes it this way: "God, who at sundry times and in divers manners spake in time past unto the fathers by the prophets, hath in these last days spoken to us by His Son" (Heb. 1:1, 2).

Written Record Needed

But what about people who were not present and so did not see God's involvement in history or the events surrounding Christ's incarnation, life, death, and resurrection? To reach *all* men, obviously, a written record was needed. God has given this to us in the Bible, through which He has revealed Himself.

The Bible consists of two sections: the Old Testament (or Covenant), consisting of 39 books, and the New Testament (or Covenant), consisting of 27 books. In the Hebrew Bible, the books of the Old Testament are arranged in three divisions — the Law, the Prophets, and the Writings.

In the Septuagint (often denoted LXX, the Roman numeral for the number of its translators), a translation of the Hebrew Old Testament into Greek made during the Third Century, B.C., the books are arranged according to similarity of subject matter. The Pentateuch (the Law, or five books of Moses) is followed by the historical books. Then come the books of poetry and wisdom and, finally, the prophets. This is the order of the books in most Christian editions of the Bible today. The writing of the Old Testament covered a span of a thousand years.

The 27 New Testament books are in four groups: the four Gospels, the Acts of the Apostles, 21 letters (epistles), and The Revelation. These books were written within the span of a century. The earliest documents were the first letters of Paul, which, along with perhaps the letter of James, were written between A.D. 48 and 60, and the Gospels and other books between A.D. 60 and 100.

How did the Bible come to be written? Two clear statements from the New Testament answer this question: "Knowing this first, that no prophecy of the Scripture is of any private interpretation. For the prophecy came not in old time by the will of man; but holy men of God spake as they were moved by the Holy Spirit" (2 Peter 1:20, 21); "All Scripture is given by inspiration of God, and is profitable for doctrine, for reproof, for correction, for instruction in righteousness" (2 Tim. 3:16).

Given by Inspiration

The Bible originated in the mind of God, not in the mind of man. It was given man by *inspiration*. It is important to understand this term, because its biblical meaning is different from that which we often give it in everyday language. The Bible is not inspired as the writings of a great novelist are inspired, or as Bach's music was inspired. Inspiration, in the biblical sense, means that God so superintended the writers of Scripture that they wrote what He wanted them to write and were kept from error in so doing. The word "inspired" (2 Tim. 3:16) actually means "outbreathed" (by God). Inspiration applies to the end result — the Scripture itself — as well as to the men whom God used to write the Scripture.

This does not mean that the human writers of Scripture were practically machines through whom God dictated. Nor does it mean that they were human typewriters whom God punched. On the contrary, their full personalities entered into their writing. Their individual writing styles are evident, for instance. Their backgrounds also are often apparent in what they wrote. But though their human capacities came into play, they were superintended and borne along in a unique way by the

Holy Spirit. Because of this, the Bible is called "The Word of God" (Mark 7:13; Heb. 4:12; etc.).

It is clear that some material in the Bible came directly from God; it could not otherwise have been known by the human mind. Genesis 1 and 2 are an example of this sort of material, which must have been made known to Moses supernaturally. In other cases, men recorded events which they themselves witnessed; e.g., John wrote about his approach, with Peter, to the empty tomb on the first Easter morning (John 20:3-10). Some writers used records that were already in existence, as Luke did in writing his Gospel (Luke 1:1-4). In other instances, God put into men's mouths the very words they should speak, or told them what to write: "The word came to Jeremiah from the Lord, saying, 'Thus speaketh the Lord God of Israel, saying, "Write thee all the words that I have spoken unto thee in a book"'" (Jer. 30:1, 2).

To say that the Scripture is inspired is not to say that all of the attitudes and ideas mentioned in the Bible are directly from God. Some of the record includes the words of evil and foolish men and even of Satan himself. Such parts are not revelation as such, nor are they the words of God, yet they are recorded in Scripture by God's intention and inspiration.

In the Book of Job, for instance, the words of Jehovah, the words of Satan, the speeches of Job's three friends, and the words of Job himself are given. All are not equally authoritative, but inspiration guarantees that what each one said was accurately recorded.

It is a striking fact that however the words came to be recorded, all Scripture is viewed by the writers as from God. Paul speaks of Scripture as "the oracles of God" (Rom. 3:2). Most significant of all, the apostles and our Lord Himself quoted the Old Testament — not merely as the counsel of a particular patriarch or prophet, but as the counsel of *God,* given through the writers: "Lord, Thou . . . by the mouth of Thy servant David hast said . . ." (Acts 4:24, 25).

Other passages speak of God as if *He* were the Scriptures. For example: "For the Scripture says to Pharaoh, 'I have raised you up for the very purpose of showing My power in you, so that My name may be proclaimed in all the earth'" (Rom. 9:17, NAS; cf. Ex. 9:16). Benjamin Warfield pointed out that these instances of the Scriptures being spoken of as if they were God, and of God being spoken of as if He were the Scriptures, could only result from a habitual identification of the text of Scripture with God speaking. It became natural to use the terms "Scripture says," and "God says," synonymously. In other words, "Scripture" and the speaking of God were seen as identical.[1]

Extent of Inspiration

The question of the extent of inspiration is frequently raised and is an important issue today. The terms *plenary* and *verbal* inspiration are used. *Plenary* means full. When used in connection with inspiration, it means that *all* of Scripture is inspired — not merely some parts. Some take the position that the only inspired (and therefore inerrant) parts of the Bible are those having to do with spiritual issues and salvation. These people maintain that to apply the claim of inspiration (and consequently inerrancy or trustworthiness) to matters involving human history or the physical world (science) is to encounter insuperable barriers.

Some scholars hold that the Bible "contains" the Word of God rather than *is* the Word of God. This view, however, confronts us with a serious problem. How can we know what parts of the Bible are trustworthy and what parts are not? How do we know which aspects have to do entirely with salvation and which are "only" matters of history? Often the two — salvation and history — are inextricably intertwined. For instance, if the Cross and the Resurrection were not historical events, of what value are they in salvation?

Moreover, if the Bible's references to the physical world and to history are not trustworthy, on what basis can we be sure that those portions dealing with salvation are trustworthy? If we are going to pick and choose the parts of the Bible we can believe, we must depend on personal subjective judgment. On matters involving eternal destiny, this is a shaky basis on which to proceed.

There have been three bases of religious authority. The first is tradition, or the authority of the Church, to which Roman Catholics have adhered. The second is human reason, which liberal thinkers have adopted. The third is the Bible itself, which evangelicals have always recognized as authoritative. To take this third position is not to deny the value of tradition and of human reason, but to submit them, in case of conflict, to the authority of Scripture.

Evangelicals do not deny that there are problems in reconciling some statements of Scripture with what historical data we possess. But the evidence of modern archaeology has, with few exceptions, confirmed the Bible record, so it would not seem unreasonable to postpone judgment on the questions still in doubt.

The term *verbal inspiration* indicates that inspiration extends to the *words* of the Bible themselves, not only to the ideas. We have already seen that God did not "dictate" the Scripture mechanically, but guided and superintended the writers within the framework of their own personalities and backgrounds. This guidance would of necessity include their choice of words, since thoughts are composed of words, much as a bar of music consists of individual notes. To alter the notes alters the music. Verbal inspiration holds that God, by His Spirit, has guaranteed the authenticity and reliability of the very words that were written, without depriving the writers of their individuality. A Christian who has a high view of inspiration is, of all people, sincerely interested in using modern tools in textual study to determine the original text.

The inspiration of which the Scripture speaks applies only to the text *as originally produced by the writers*. There have been some errors in copying, though they are fewer and less significant than one would think.

We have observed that the Bible *is* the Word of God; it does not merely *contain* the Word of God, as many believe. Others say the Bible *becomes* the Word of God to an individual when the person has an "existential encounter" with God in his reading of Scripture — when the Truth of a passage makes a powerful and indelible impression on him. Those who hold this position are often in strong reaction to "dead" orthodoxy — to the profession of evangelical beliefs unaccompanied by evidence of the believer's having been changed by God's power.

Holy Spirit Illuminates

Scripture must be illumined in the heart of an individual by the Holy Spirit before it becomes meaningful to him. Before the coming of the Spirit, at Pentecost, the Father and the Son had revealed divine truth. When Peter answered our Lord's climactic question, "Who do you say I am?" with, "Thou art the Christ, the Son of the living God," Jesus said, "Blessed art thou, Simon Bar-Jona, for flesh and blood hath not revealed it unto thee, but *My Father* which is in heaven" (Matt. 16:15-17). When Jesus was talking to the two disciples on the road to Emmaus after His resurrection, *He* "expounded unto them in all the Scriptures the things concerning Himself." As He sat with them, "their eyes were opened, and they knew Him" (Luke 24:27, 31). "Then opened *He* their understanding, that they might understand the Scriptures" (24:

45). In telling the disciples about His going away, He said, "Howbeit when He, the Spirit of truth [the Holy Spirit], is come, He will guide you into all truth" (John 16:13).

Paul speaks of God's revealing by the Spirit what He has prepared for those who love Him (1 Cor. 2:9, 10). The illuminating work of the Spirit of God is necessary if we are to know *anything* about God. What the Holy Spirit illumines is "the Sword of the Spirit, which is the Word of God" (Eph. 6:17). It does not *become* the Word of God; it *is* the Word of God.

A television set, sitting in the corner but not turned on, is still a television set. I won't get any images or sound until I turn it on, but it *is* a television set, whether turned on or not. It doesn't *become* a television set when turned on.

So, too, the Scripture *is* the Word of God, whether anybody ever responds to it or not. The Holy Spirit must illumine Scripture in a person's heart before it becomes *meaningful,* but what He illumines *is* the Word of God, not something less. It doesn't *become* something it wasn't before.

Having seen that the Bible *is* the Word of God, we must now consider the principles of interpreting and understanding it. Considerable confusion has resulted because people have oversimplified the kinds of biblical interpretation as either "literal" or "figurative." Those who take the Bible literally are made to look foolish by their apparent denial of any use of figures of speech in the Bible. Those, on the other hand, who take it figuratively often appear to be capricious in evading the clear meaning of statements they do not want to accept.

The fact is that some parts of the Bible are to be taken literally and other parts figuratively.

The key question is, What did the writer intend his readers to understand? We must ask to whom the passage was written. Is the promise or command, for instance, one that has universal application or one that has limited reference? Often there are primary and secondary applications. A primary application has to do with the person or people directly addressed. A secondary application relates a scriptural principle to those to whom the passage is not applied directly.

It is important to consider the context in which a Bible statement is made. What is the primary teaching of the passage? Statements must not be lifted out of context in such a way as to cause misunderstanding. A skeptic once triumphantly asserted, "The Bible says, 'There is no God.'" He was considerably deflated when reminded of the context: "The fool hath said in his heart, 'There is no God'" (Ps. 14:1).

Literal or Figurative?

It is important to decide whether a statement is literal or figurative. The Bible uses such literary forms as poetry, allegory, and parable. Though there are passages on which there is strong difference of opinion, it is usually no more difficult to distinguish between figurative and literal statements in the Bible than in a daily newspaper.

The statement, "Two people were killed in an accident on Main Street," is obviously literal. "He shot home from third in the last half of the ninth with the winning run under his arm, and the crowd went mad," is readily recognized as figurative language. A player does not "shoot" home or carry runs under his arm. And the folks in the bleachers, though they may get excited, do not become insane.

A final word about Bible study. Simply using a dictionary to investigate the full meaning of the words of Scripture will reveal surprising riches. Try it! And consult several translations.

It has been said that the Scripture is its own best commentary. Often a verse or a passage becomes clear when studied in the light of other Bible statements on the same subject. Though humanly the Bible has many writers, in the final analysis there was only one Author — God Himself. As we compare Scripture with Scripture, we are guarded against becoming unbalanced in our views. We need to study individual books and we also need to trace themes through the whole Bible. This is the difference between biblical theology and systematic theology. One scholar compares biblical theology to "the profusion of nature in which the various plants and flowers are scattered with a bountiful hand in 'ordered disorder.'" He compared systematic theology to a botanical garden "where plants and flowers are gathered and arranged according to species."[2] Both kinds of arrangements are useful; both have their place in a study of botany. Both kinds of Bible study are useful, too.

The Canon of Scripture

A separate question from that of inspiration is that of the canon, i.e., *which* writings, or books, are recognized as *inspired?* It is important to realize that a book did not become inspired by being included in the canon. Inclusion in the canon was merely recognition of the authority the book already possessed.

We do not know exactly when the Old Testament canon was completed. The Old Testament itself says that collections of "authorized" books were put in the sacred buildings — the Tabernacle and then the Temple. Hilkiah rediscovered the Book of the Law there (2 Kings 22). The Jews recognized as their Scriptures certain books that recorded Jehovah's dealings with Israel.

In our Lord's time, the Old Testament was viewed as a completed collection. He and the apostles referred to this collection as "the Scripture." Most of the books of the Old Testament are quoted in the New Testament, always as authoritative.

In tracing the canonicity of a particular book — that is, its recognition as one of the inspired writings — we must keep three questions in mind: (1) Is it mentioned by the Early Church fathers in the Christian literature of the first centuries of our era? (2) What attitude do these early writers take toward the inspiration of the book? (3) Do they regard it as part of a canon, or list of books recognized as inspired?

The definition of the canon was important, in the Early Church, because claims were being advanced for many writings which were patently spurious, and because heretics were attacking the validity of the genuine Scriptures. The canon, as we know it today, became fixed in the Fourth Century. Athanasius (A.D. 297-373), known as the father of orthodoxy, became patriarch of Alexandria. In his 39th Paschal Letter (A.D. 367), he listed the books of the New Testament as we know them.

The canon of the New Testament was also confirmed at a Church Council held in Carthage in A.D. 397. The Council used three criteria in recognizing canonicity. First, Was a book apostolic in origin? Mark and Luke were accepted, for example, because they were recognized as the work of close associates of the apostles. Second, was the book used and recognized by the churches? Third, did the book teach sound doctrine?[3]

It is on these bases that the orthodox Protestant Church today does not receive as canonical the 12 books of the Apocrypha (1 and 2 Maccabees, 1 and 2 Esdras, Tobit, Judith, Wisdom of Solomon, Ecclesiasticus, Baruch, Song of the Three Holy Children, Susanna, Bel and the Dragon, and the Prayer of Manasses), which the Roman Catholic Church accepts. The Jews never recognized these books as part of their Old Testament.

To accept the Bible as the Word of God today is not fashionable. Some, even within the professing Church, deny its reliability. Generally, attacks on

Scripture follow certain lines. Perhaps the foremost is that of contending that the Bible is incompatible with 20th Century science. Many conflicts are said to exist between scientific facts and statements in the Bible. There are, admittedly, some problems. But the following considerations usually bridge what on first sight may seem a yawning chasm.

Understanding the Bible

First, the Bible speaks in *phenomenological* language — that is, it describes things *as they appear to be* rather than in precise scientific terms. To say the sun rises in the east is a phenomenological statement. Technically, we know the sun does not really "rise," but even the *Naval Almanac* uses the term "sunrise," and we would not charge the Almanac with error. The Bible has been understandable in all cultures and throughout history because of the phenomenological way it describes things. It does not claim to be textbook on science, but where it touches scientific matters, it does not give misinformation.

Second, when Bible information is incomplete, it is not necessarily incorrect. Science is always building on previous knowledge. Advancement on incomplete theories does not mean the theories were incorrect.

Third, we must always guard against making the Bible say things which, on closer examination, it really doesn't say. And it is most important to determine whether, in a given instance, the Bible is speaking figuratively or literally.

21

Fourth, we must carefully investigate to see whether the supposed conflict is between biblical teaching and scientific facts or simply between an *interpretation* of Scripture and an *interpretation* of the facts. Often an interpretation at variance with biblical truth is more philosophic than scientific.

Fifth, it would be foolish to "freeze" the points of conflict and assume the Bible wrong. The Bible has not changed in 2,000 years, but science admittedly is a moving train. To have reconciled the Bible to scientific views current a century ago would have been to make Scripture obsolete today! Far better to *admit* an apparent conflict and await the development of additional evidence.

That there is no basic conflict between science and Scripture is suggested by the fact that modern science was born and developed largely by earnest Christians. Believing in a personal God as Creator, they were convinced that the universe was orderly and therefore capable of meaningful investigation. In scientific research they felt they were thinking God's thoughts after Him. There can be no ultimate conflict between truth of biblical revelation and that discovered by science, for all truth is from God and is therefore consistent. In our day, when some 90 percent of all scientists who have ever lived are alive, many outstanding scientists are also earnest Christians.

Dating Problems Explained

In another line of attack it is contended that the Bible is not reliable historically and that there are "internal" contradictions in parallel accounts of the same event. Some apparent numerical errors may be due to mistakes in transmission of the text over many years. Recent archaeological discoveries, however, show that the ancients' system of dating explains many numerical problems. If one king, for example, ended his rule and another began ruling in a given calendar year, *both* were given credit for ruling the entire year. Also, it is important to remember that the biblical writers often used round figures which, though not precise, are at the same time not incorrect.

Admittedly we do not presently have complete explanations for all seeming Bible discrepancies. But it would be unscientific, in the light of modern archaeological discoveries, to adopt the prevalent assumption that the Bible is wrong until proven right, rather than the reverse. Dr. W. F. Albright, one of the world's leading archaeologists, has said, "There can be no doubt that archaeology has confirmed the substantial historicity of the Old Testament tradition."[4]

Nelson Glueck, famed Jewish archaeologist, writes, "It may be stated categorically that no archaeological discovery has ever controverted a biblical reference."[5]

We do not "prove" the Bible by archaeology. The Holy Spirit confirms in our hearts the conviction that the Bible is the Word of God. But it is gratifying to know that scientific evidence is consistent with Scripture.

We can with confidence affirm, with the hymn writer:

The Bible stands like a rock undaunted
    'Mid the raging storms of time;
Its pages burn with the truth eternal,
    And they glow with a light sublime.
The Bible stands though the hills may tumble;
    It will firmly stand when the earth shall crumble;
I will plant my feet on its firm foundation,
        For the Bible stands!

                    Haldor Lillenas

"Forever, O Lord, Thy Word is settled in heaven" (Ps. 119:89).

For Further Reading

Bruce, F. F. *The New Testament Documents: Are They Reliable?* Chicago: Inter-Varsity Press, 1960.

Henry, C. F. H., ed. *Revelation and the Bible.* Grand Rapids: Baker Book House, 1958.

Mickelsen, A. B. *Interpreting the Bible.* Grand Rapids: Wm. B. Eerdmans Co., 1963.

Packer, J. I. *Fundamentalism and the Word of God.* Grand Rapids: Wm. B. Eerdmans Co., 1958.

Ramm, Bernard. *The Christian View of Science and Scripture.* Grand Rapids: Wm. B. Eerdmans Co., 1955.

Chapter 2

God

"What we believe about God," said the late A. W. Tozer, "is the most important thing about us." Our belief or lack of it inevitably translates itself into our actions and attitudes.

It is interesting, on the basis of how Joseph reacted to his traitorous brothers and to his unjust imprisonment for refusing the seduction of Potiphar's wife, to reconstruct the God Joseph believed in. Moses, because of the God he trusted, "endured as seeing Him who is invisible" (Heb. 11:27). He gave up the king's palace for the desert and God's people. Significantly, faith, in Hebrews 11, is illustrated by what people *did* rather than what they *said* or professed.

The word "God" is one of the most widely used — but vague and undefined — terms in our language. Some people, such as Einstein, think of God as "a pure mathematical mind." Others see Him as a shadowy superhuman person or force.

Still others see God as a ball of fire to which we, as sparks of life, will ultimately be reunited — or as a celestial policeman. A few think of Him as a sentimental grandfather of the sky.

Increasing godlessness causes some people to urge us to agree simply to use the word "God" without even trying to define it lest we breed division. It is obvious, however, that if God *is*, His existence and His nature do not depend on what anyone thinks about Him. To conceive of God as a stone idol or as a mystical idea does not *make* Him either. If I am interested in *reality*, I must know what God is *really* like. This I cannot know apart from His revealing Himself to me. How God has done this is summed up by the writer to the Hebrews: "God . . . at sundry times in divers manners spake in time past unto the fathers by the prophets . . . [and] hath in these last days spoken unto us by His Son" (Heb. 1:1, 2).

Because God has spoken and has revealed Himself, we no longer have the need or the option of conjuring up ideas and images of God by our own imaginations. Our personal concept of God — when we pray, for instance — is *worthless* unless it coincides with His revelation of Himself.

God's "Natural" Attributes

The terms that describe the nature of God — love, holiness, sovereignty, etc. — are known as His attributes. They are classified as "natural" attributes and "moral" attributes. Let's think first about God's "natural" attributes, as revealed by His self-disclosure in Scripture.

First, God is separate from His creation. He is *transcendent* — above and beyond His creation, the heavens and the earth. He is not a slave to natural law He authored, but is independent of it and above it. He can override it at will — though normally He does not interfere with it. He is exalted and eternal, the world's Creator, Sovereign, and Judge.

But God is *immanent* as well as transcendent. By this we mean that His presence and power pervade His entire creation. He does not stand apart from the world, a mere spectator of the things He has made.

The prophet spoke of God's *transcendence* when he wrote of "the high and lofty One that inhabiteth eternity, whose name is Holy [set apart]," and of His *immanence* when he spoke of Him as the One who dwells "with him also that is of a contrite and humble spirit" (Isa. 57:15).

God is not so totally transcendent that He set the universe in motion and then left it, as Deists would have us believe. Nor is He so immanent that He is indistinguishable from the universe. Pantheism holds that God is all and that all is God. But that means you and I would be part of God, which ultimately means that God sins when we sin. If all is God, and everything else is illusion, as some hold, then what could exist to *have* the illusion? Does God have illusions?

One who sees God in nature is not necessarily a pantheist. The Bible itself tells us that the universe which God has made speaks to us of His eternal power (*omnipotence*) and Deity (cf. Rom.

1:19, 20). The Rocky Mountains, Niagara Falls, the starry hosts of heaven, the ocean's vastness — all remind us that God made them and is sovereign over them.

The prophet observed, "Oh, Lord God . . . there is nothing too hard for Thee" (Jer. 32:17), and the Angel Gabriel assured Mary, after informing her of her privilege of bearing the Son of God as a virgin, "For with God nothing shall be impossible" (Luke 1:37).

The omnipotence of God is limited by his moral character. For example, though "nothing [is] impossible" with God, He cannot lie (Heb. 6:18). His omnipotence applies to inherent possibilities, not inherent impossibilities. Someone has asked, "Is it possible for God to make anything too heavy for Himself to lift? If not, can we say He is omnipotent?" Nonsense is still nonsense, as C. S. Lewis says, whether we are talking about something else or about God.

God's Eternity

God is *eternal* — that is, He never had a beginning and will never have an end. He is the "One who inhabiteth eternity" (Isa. 57:15). "The eternal God is our refuge" (Deut. 33:27). From everlasting to everlasting, He is God (cf. Ps. 90: 2). He is not a prisoner of time, because time — as we know it — began with Creation. The answer to the question, "Who created God?" is, "No one and nothing," because God is completely self-existent. There was never a time when He did not exist.

God is *infinite*. By this we mean that He is not limited by or confined to the universe. He is entirely independent of finite (measurable) things and beings. There have been times when God has put limitations on Himself, as when He appeared to Old Testament believers in the form of an angel or a man (e.g., Gen. 18:1) and when He became incarnate in the person of Jesus Christ. He imposed such limitation on Himself in order to bless His creatures, not because He *had* to.[6]

It has been pointed out that our minds cannot adequately conceive of an *infinite* quantity of anything — space, power, potatoes. Such a concept baffles and frustrates us. We *can*, however, imagine a being — God — who is infinite in the sense that He has no limitations. God's infinite holiness does not mean that He has a boundless *amount* of holiness — for holiness cannot be measured in this way. Rather, it means that His holiness has no limitations and no defeats. The same may be said for each of His other attributes.

God's infinity is also a matter of "boundless activity," — that is, His power (omnipotence) is at work in and in control of everything, anywhere, that exists.[7]

God is *unchangeable*. With Him "no variation occurs, nor shadow cast by turning" (James 1:17, BERK). It is important that we not think of God in terms of human personality, which is ordinarily volatile and unsteady. God's love is steadfast and constant, and is not subject to the ebbs and flows of human love. His wrath is a fixed attitude toward sin and is not like our fits of temper when something displeases us.

A man who walks east into a strong east wind, and then turns around and walks west, would say, "The wind *was* on my face, but *now* it is on my back." But there would have been no change in the wind. His *direction* was what changed, and this change brought him into a new relationship with the wind. God never changes, and when He *seems* to be different it is because *we* have changed and in so doing have come into a different relationship toward Him.

When God "Repents"

The Bible speaks of God as *repenting* (changing His mind). The term describes what *seems* to us to have happened. As an instance, God threatened to destroy the ancient city of Nineveh, but after Jonah had preached there the people turned to God for forgiveness and He is said to have repented (Jonah 3:10) of His plan to destroy them. Actually, the Ninevites had turned from rebellion to repentance, and so they came under God's mercy and forgiveness instead of His wrath. God Himself had not changed.

God is *omnipresent,* which means He is fully present everywhere. He is not like a substance spread out in a thin layer all over the earth — *all* of Him is in Chicago, in Calcutta, in Cairo, and in Caracas, at one and the same time.

God is *omniscient* — that is, He knows everything, including our own thoughts. "Thou understandest my thought afar off" (Ps. 139:2), David wrote about God, and the Apostle John wrote of our Lord that He needed no testimony from anyone about [men], for He well knew what was in human nature" (John 2:25, WMS). Moreover, He declares the end from the beginning (Isa. 46:10), and nothing takes Him by surprise.

Jesus declared that God is *a Spirit* and that those who worship Him must do so in [the] Spirit and in truth (John 4:24). God does not have a physical body. When we speak of the "hand of God" or the "nostrils of God" we are using "anthropomorphisms" — human expressions — to describe God, though we know they are not *literally* true.

We have saved for last the fact about God which, among His "natural" attributes, is of the greatest importance. God is all-powerful, all-wise, infinite and eternal, and changeless, and we are not to think of Him as an impersonal force behind the universe. God is *personal* — that is, He is a Person. He has the elements of personality — intellect, feelings, and will. He is self-determining — as, within our limitations, we also are. He does according to His own purpose and will.

We know this of God because He created man in His own image and after His own likeness (Gen. 1:26). Since *we* are persons, God cannot possibly be something less than a person. What is created cannot be of a higher order than its Creator.

Because God is personal, we know that His sovereign will is not akin to the blind fate ("Kismet") of Islam's Allah. It is, rather, the loving purpose of a heavenly Father to whom His children are precious. And because God is a Person and we are persons, communication between Him and us is possible.

God's Moral Attributes

God's other qualities are called His "moral" attributes. It is not enough to know merely that God exists; it is desperately important to know about His moral nature. Suppose we knew God existed, but thought He was like Adolf Hitler. What a horrible truth to contemplate, and what a heinous existence we would have!

Holiness is perhaps the most comprehensive of all of God's attributes. "It is a term for the moral excellence of God and His freedom from all limitation in His moral perfection. 'Thou art of purer eyes than to behold evil' (Hab. 1:13)."[8] In this exalted sense, only God is holy. He is therefore the standard of ethical purity by which His creatures must measure themselves.

"Since holiness embraces every distinctive attribute of the Godhead, it may be defined as the outshining of all that God is. As the sun's rays, combining all the colors of the spectrum, come together in the sun's shining and blend into light, so in His self-manifestation all the attributes of God come together and blend into holiness. Holiness has, for that reason, been called 'an attribute of attributes' — that which lends unity to all the attributes of God. To conceive of God's being and character as merely a [collection] of abstract perfectness is to deprive God of all reality."⁹ Holiness is the sum total of the perfections of the God of the Bible

All the attributes of God are in perfect harmony and are in no way antagonistic to each other. God's love and mercy are not opposed to, or exercised at the expense of, His righteousness and holiness. Sometimes it is wrongly suggested that the God of the Old Testament is a God of wrath and anger, but that in the New Testament we have God in Christ portrayed as love and gentleness. The implication is sometimes drawn that these are two different Gods. This, of course, is completely false. The God of the Old Testament, who repeatedly had mercy on the Israelites after they repented, is the same God who wept over Jerusalem because her people killed the prophets and would not turn to the Lord. The Jesus who spoke frequently of hell and eternal judgment is the same God who moved in judgment on Jerusalem in 586 B.C., and on the pagan Belshazzar some years later.

Our Triune God

At the heart of the Christian view of God is the concept of the *Trinity*. Rather than being "excess baggage," as former Episcopal Bishop James A. Pike called it, this truth is central to an understanding of biblical revelation and the Christian Gospel. Departure from the doctrine of the Trinity has been and is one of the major sources of heresy in the Christian Church.

The term "Trinity" does not occur in the Bible, but this does not mean that the idea is a later development or one that is a product of philosophic speculation rather than divine revelation.

The Trinity is a difficult concept, not fully susceptible to human explanation, because it involves categories which our finite mental powers cannot grasp. Anyone who has ever tried to explain the Trinity to an unbeliever will agree that it could hardly be a human invention. It is a teaching which God Himself has revealed to us.

The doctrine is that "God is one in His essential being, but that the 'divine essence' exists in three modes or forms, each constituting a Person, yet in such a way that the divine essence is wholly in each Person."[10] God is one Being, but He exists in three Persons.

The first Old Testament clue concerning the Trinity comes in the story of creation. God (Elohim) created by means of the Word and the Spirit (Gen. 1:1-3). These immortal words were read by Commander Frank Borman in Apollo 8 as the spacecraft circled the moon: "In the beginning God created the heaven and the earth. And the earth was without form, and void, and darkness was upon the face of the deep. And the Spirit of God moved upon the face of the waters. And God said, Let there be light, and there was light."

"Here we are introduced . . . to the Word as a personal creative power, and to the Spirit as the bringer of life and order to the creation. There is revealed thus early a threefold center of activity. God, as Creator, thought out the Universe, expressed His thought in a Word, and made His Spirit its animating principle."[11]

Some believe that when God (Elohim) said, "Let Us make man in Our image" (Gen. 1:26), the plural forms used (Elohim, us, our) are to be understood as a revelation of the Trinity by God to man, and that man's awareness of this truth was later lost through the Fall.

Other indications of the Trinity are to be found in Genesis 48:15, 16; Exodus 31:3; Numbers 11:25; Judges 3:10; Proverbs 8:22-31 (the Word is here personified as Wisdom); and Isaiah 11:2; 42:1; 61:1. In these passages the Spirit is clearly the source of blessing, power, and strength.

The Bible's emphasis throughout, however, is on the fact that God is *one*. "Hear, O Israel: the Lord our God is one Lord" (Deut. 6:4). This truth was in sharp contrast to the rampant polytheism that surrounded the nation of Israel. We must not allow the scriptural truth of the Trinity to deprive us of the equally important teaching that there is only *one* God.

It is both interesting and significant that in the New Testament, where the distinctness of the persons of the Godhead is more clear, the disciples were taught by our Lord to baptize in *the name*, singular, of the Father and of the Son and of the Holy Spirit (Matt. 28:19).

John the Baptist spoke of the coming baptism of the (Holy) Spirit, of which his own water baptism was a symbol. When John baptized Him, Jesus saw "the heavens opened and the Spirit like a dove descending upon Him. And there came a voice from heaven saying, Thou art My beloved Son, in whom I am well pleased" (Mark 1:10, 11).

This was a clear manifestation of the Trinity, all of the three Persons of the Godhead being referred to.

Earlier, at the birth of Jesus, all three Persons of the Godhead are also mentioned. The angel told Mary that her child would be the *Son* of *God* conceived by the *Holy Spirit* (Luke 1:35).

Jesus explicitly spoke of the Father and the Spirit as being distinct Persons from Himself (John 14; 16).

Salvation itself portrays the work of the triune God. The Father sent the Son to accomplish the work of redemption. The Son sent the Spirit to bring conviction and to apply to men what Christ had accomplished.

The apostolic benediction, "The grace of the Lord Jesus Christ, and the love of God, and the communion of the Holy Spirit, be with you all" (2 Cor. 13:14), is another instance of apostolic teaching on the Trinity.

Each person of the Trinity is fully God. Paul wrote of "God our Father" (Rom. 1:7), and spoke of Christ as the "dear Son . . . who is the image of the invisible God" (Col. 1:13, 15) and as "God our Saviour" (Tit. 3:4).

The deity of the Holy Spirit is also clear. Peter told Ananias that in lying to the Holy Spirit, he had "not lied unto men, but unto God" (Acts 5: 3, 4).

A Semantic Problem

Part of the problem of understanding the Trinity is the inadequacy of human words to express divine reality. For instance, we speak of the "Persons" in the Godhead. We use this term because it describes a being who has intellect, emotion, and will. We can understand this. But we must be careful in applying such terms to God. "In most [cases] the doctrine is stated by saying that God is one in His essential being, but that in this being there are three Persons, yet so as not to form separate and distinct individuals. They are three modes or forms in which the divine essence exists. 'Person' is, however, an imperfect expression of the truth, inasmuch as the term denotes to us a *separate* rational and moral individual. But in the being of God there are not three *individuals*, but only three *personal self distinctions* within the one divine essence.

"Then again, personality in man implies independence of will, actions, and feelings, leading to behavior peculiar to the [individual]. This cannot be thought of in connection with the Trinity: each Person is self-conscious and self-directing, yet never acts independently or in opposition [to the others]. When we say that God is a Unity, we mean that though [He] is in Himself a threefold center of life, His life is not split into three. He is one in essence, in personality, and in will. When we say that God is a Trinity in Unity, we mean that there is unity in diversity, and that diversity manifests itself in Persons, in characteristics, and in operations."[12]

Just as the word "person" is not exact when applied to the Godhead, but is the best approximation available, so it is with the word "substance."

The Trinity was spoken of in the Early Church as "three Persons in one Substance." But here "substance is, of course, immaterial; it must not be thought of either as a common spiritual 'stuff' or 'material' out of which three Beings of the same divine nature are produced (as we talk of silver as the *substance* from which coins may be made). The divine essence is not *divided* into three: it is fully present in each of the Persons. 'Substance' thus relates to the one Being who is God, rather than to the nature or being of that God."[13]

It is also important to understand the relationships of the Persons of the Trinity. The Son and the Spirit are said to be "subordinate" to the Father, but this does not mean they are inferior. Their subordination has been called a matter of relationship, but not of nature.

"The Father, as the fount of Deity, is first. He is said to *originate*. The Son, eternally begotten of the Father, is second. He is said to *reveal*. The Spirit, eternally proceeding from the Father and the Son, is third. He is said to *execute*. . . . Thus we can say that creation is from the Father, through the Son, by the Holy Spirit."[14]

The Spirit of God is said to proceed from the Son as well as from the Father. The Father is the one by whom the Son is begotten and from whom the Spirit proceeds.

Two Major Heresies

There have been two major heretical distortions of the Trinity, and they exist at present. One is an attempt to get away from any implication that there are three separate and distinct Persons in the Godhead. Originating with a man named Sabellius in the Third Century, this error claims that Father, Son and Holy Spirit are merely different manifestations of the one God which He assumes temporarily to achieve His purposes. At times God appears as Father, at times as Son, and at times as the Holy Spirit, say the Sabellians.

The other emphasis was originated by Arius (about A.D. 325). Though Arius emphasized the unity of God, he so stressed the Persons of the Trinity that he ended up by dividing the substance of the Godhead. "This resulted chiefly from his definition of the Son and the Holy Spirit as being lesser, subordinate Beings whom the Father willed into existence for the purpose of acting as His agents in His dealings with the world and men. In effect, Arius reduced our Lord (and the Spirit) below the level of strict Deity." He would admit (Christ's) Deity in a secondary sense, but denied His *eternal* Sonship. He admitted that Christ existed before the foundation of the world, but denied that He was coeternal with the Father. The disciples of Arius, by teaching that the Spirit was brought into existence by the Son, reduced Him to a lesser form of Deity.

In more recent times, some movements, such as Unitarianism, Russellism (Jehovah's Witnesses), and Mormonism assign our Lord and the Holy Spirit a nature and position below that of true Deity. "This is one of the most important battlegrounds in the history of the Church, and no true

Christian should for one moment tolerate any description of our Master other than that which assigns to Him the fullest Deity, co-equal and co-eternal with the Father."[15]

It is also important that we know about God's providence and will if our knowledge of God is to be accurate. He is not only the Creator of the universe — He is also its Sustainer in the physical sense, and is the moral Governor of the intelligent beings He has created. The sweep of God's providence and sovereignty are complete and comprehensive. "Whatsoever the Lord pleased, that did He in heaven, and in earth, in the seas, and all deep places" (Ps. 135:6). This truth is echoed in the New Testament: "For to do whatsoever Thy hand and Thy counsel determined before to be done" (Acts 4:28). God is the One in whom "all things hold together" (cf. Col. 1:17, NAS). He is the One "who worketh all things after the counsel of His own will" (Eph. 1:11).

God's Decrees

God's control of the universe is often spoken of in terms of His *decrees*. Someone has defined the decrees of God as that eternal plan by which God makes sure that all the events of the universe — past, present, and future — take place. To our finite, limited minds there appear to be a great many events, but with God there is no time and everything happens in one eternal moment. This is why we say God knows the end from the beginning.

A distinction is sometimes made between the absolute *decrees* of God, which determine what happens, and His *purposes* for His creatures — that is, His revelation to them of their duties. God's decrees are always accomplished, but men frequently ignore and disobey His purposes for them.

Another distinction is made between the *directive* will and the *permissive* will of God. His directive will is what He brings to pass; His permissive will is what he allows to take place. God *permitted*, but did not *direct*, the entrance of sin into the world. But whether actively (by decree) or passively (by permission), God is sovereign over all that happens. He is *free* in that He is under no other influence or power of anything or anyone but Himself. "Who hath directed the Spirit of the Lord, or being His counselor hath taught Him?" (Isa. 40:13) He is *sovereign* — He has power to bring His purposes to pass.

What About Free Will?

The question of God's sovereignty and its relation to human freedom troubles many people. If God directs everything, how can man be a free agent and therefore morally responsible? If God knows in advance what man is going to do, what choice has he in the matter? Admittedly there are profound aspects to this question which are not altogether clear, but it is helpful to keep several things in mind:

First, man's will is always a relatively small part of any given circumstance. Man has no control over where he is born, into what family, or with what abilities or disabilities, advantages or disadvantages. He is subject to many influences beyond his control. He is rather like a baby in a playpen. He has real freedom, but only within certain prescribed bounds. Francis Schaeffer points out that when someone throws a man a ball, he can either catch it or let it fall. Barring some physical defect, he is not so limited that he has no power of decision or choice.

Second, God's foreknowledge (which is not to be confused with His election or with predestination) is not in itself the *cause* of what happens. For example, God foreknew that Demas would forsake the Apostle Paul for love of this world, but God's foreknowledge did not *predispose* Demas to turn back, much less *compel* him to do so. Demas acted in freedom; he made his own personal choice, under no compulsion.

Again, God foreknew that Saul would receive Christ and become Paul the Apostle, but on the Damascus Road Saul exercised his own will in answering the Lord's summons. God foreknows your decisions before you make them — He knows what you will do and where you will go — but this foreknowledge does not interfere in the slightest with your complete freedom to act.

Packer calls this difficulty — reconciling divine sovereignty and human freedom — an *antinomy* — an apparent contradiction between conclusions that seem equally logical, reasonable, or necessary. He says, "An antinomy exists when a pair of principles stand side by side, seemingly irreconcilable, yet both undeniable. There are cogent reasons for believing each of them: each rests on clear, solid evidence; but it is a mystery to you how they can be squared with each other. You see that each must be true on its own, but you do not see how they can both be true together. . . .

"Modern physics faces an antinomy, in this sense, in its study of light. There is cogent evidence to show that light consists of waves, and equally cogent evidence to show that it consists of particles. It is not apparent how light can be both waves and particles, but the evidence is there, and so neither view can be ruled out in favor of the other. Neither, however, can be reduced to the other or explained in terms of the other; the two seemingly incompatible positions must be held together, and both must be treated as true. Such a necessity scandalizes our tidy minds, no doubt, but there is no help for it if we are to be loyal to the facts."[16]

We may take comfort that divine sovereignty is exercised by a personal, all-loving, all-knowing God. But His sovereignty in no way lessens our freedom — or our privilege and responsibility to know and do His good will.

For Further Reading

Orr, James. *A Christian View of God and the World.* New York: Charles Scribner's Sons, 1908.

Schaeffer, Francis. *The God Who Is There.* Chicago: Inter-Varsity Press, 1968.

Chapter 3

Jesus Christ

Dr. W. H. Griffith Thomas wrote a book entitled *Christianity Is Christ*. This title sums up the heart and uniqueness of Christianity.

Buddha is not essential to the teaching of Buddhism, or Mohammed to Islam, but everything about Christianity is determined by the person and work of Jesus Christ. Christianity owes its life and character in every detail to Christ. Its teachings are teachings about Him. He was the origin and will be the fulfillment of its hopes. He is the source of its ideas, which were born of what He said and did. The strength of Christ's Church is the strength of His own Spirit, who is omnipotent.

But who is this Man, Jesus Christ? He Himself made His identity the central question of His ministry: "But whom say ye that I am?" (Matt. 16: 15). To be wrong at this point is fatal, as the history of the Church has shown.

We must be clear, first, that Jesus Christ was

fully God. He is expressly called God in various passages of Scripture, of which the following are a few examples: "The Word was God" (John 1:1; that the Word is Christ is confirmed in v. 14); "the great God and our Saviour Jesus Christ" (Titus 2:13); "His Son Jesus Christ. This is the true God" (1 John 5:20).

Christ Claimed Deity

Jesus claimed Deity for Himself in a way quite clear to His listeners. He said, on one occasion, "I and the Father are one" (John 10:30). His claim to Deity was considered by the religious leaders to be blasphemy, and led to His crucifixion: "We have a law, and by our law He ought to die, because He made Himself the Son of God" (John 19:7). The high priest expressly asked Christ, "Tell us whether Thou be the Christ, the Son of God," and Jesus answered, "Thou hast said" (Matt. 26:63, 64). This was a clear affirmative answer, and the high priest said there was no further need of witnesses because they had heard His "blasphemy" with their own ears. He had said "that God was His Father, making Himself equal with God" (John 5:18).

Jesus Christ claimed the prerogatives and authority of God. He said He had authority to forgive sins (Mark 2:10) and that He would come in the clouds of heaven, sitting at the right hand of power (Mark 14:62), implying authority to judge men: "For the Father judgeth no man, but hath committed all judgment unto the Son" (John 5:

22). Several times Jesus asserted that He Himself had the authority and power to raise the dead (John 6:39, 40, 54; 10:17, 18).

Jesus possessed attributes which belong to God alone. He claimed omnipotence, or all power (Matt. 28:18), and during His life He demonstrated this power over nature by stilling the stormy waves (Mark 4:39) and by turning water into wine (John 2:7-11); over physical disease (Mark 3:10); over the spirit world of demons (Luke 4:35); and over death by raising Lazarus from the grave (John 11:43, 44). He has also been designated as having power over all the heavenly hosts (Eph. 1:20-22).

He is omniscient, or all-knowing. He knew, as only God could know, what was in men's minds before they spoke (Mark 2:8; John 2:25). He was omnipresent, and promised to be with all His disciples to the end of the age (Matt. 28:20).

Christ the Creator

He is the Creator (John 1:3) and Sustainer (Heb. 1:3) of the universe. Perhaps the most comprehensive statement about the Deity of Christ is that "in Him dwelleth all the fulness of the Godhead bodily" (Col. 2:9).

Christ accepted the worship of men, which is due to God alone. He commended rather than rebuked doubting Thomas, who fell at His feet and declared in awe, "My Lord and my God!" (John 20:28, BERK) This was the same Jesus who scorned Satan's invitation to worship him by replying, "Thou shalt worship the Lord thy God, and Him only shalt thou serve" (Matt. 4:10; cf. Deut. 6:13).

Another dimension of Christ's Deity to be kept in mind is His preexistence. He did not *become* the Son of God, either at His birth or sometime during His earthly life. He *was* and *is* the eternal Son, coexistent and coeternal with the Father. John declared, "In the beginning was the Word," and, "without Him was not anything made that was made" (John 1:1, 3). Jesus made clear reference to His own preexistence when the Jews challenged Him concerning His age. "You're not 50 years old yet," they said; and He replied, "Before Abraham was, I am" (cf. John 8:57, 58).

The Deity of Christ is woven into the warp and woof of everything He said and taught. It is confirmed by what others clearly understood Him to say. The things that He did were conclusive evidence that His words were not clever deceit or the babblings of a demented person.

Christ Also Fully Man

But Jesus was not only fully God — He was also fully man, fully human. This is a vital aspect of the person of Christ. If He were not fully human, He could not have represented us on the cross and He could not be the High Priest who comforts and strengthens us. But He *has* gone through our human experience (Heb. 2:16-18) and is fully able to understand us and sympathize with us.

Though His conception was supernatural, Jesus'

birth was that of a normal child born of a human mother (Matt. 1:18). He is spoken of as being born of the seed of the woman (Gen. 3:15) and of the seed of Abraham (Heb. 2:16). In this way, in the Virgin Birth, "The Word became flesh" (John 1:14, NAS).

Jesus, as a normal child, grew physically and mentally. "And the Child grew, and waxed strong in spirit, filled with wisdom . . . and Jesus increased in wisdom and stature, and in favor with God and man" (Luke 2:40, 52).

Jesus referred to Himself as a man: "Ye seek to kill Me, a man that hath told you the truth" (John 8:40). He was recognized by others as a man (Acts 2:22). He had a body, soul, and spirit, and shared our physical and emotional experiences.

Jesus got hungry (Matt. 4:2) and thirsty (John 19:28). His feet ached and He got weary from traveling (John 4:6). He needed sleep and refreshment (Matt. 8:24). He experienced and expressed love and compassion (Matt. 9:36). He was angry at those who defiled His Father's house (Matt. 21:13) and who deliberately refused the truth of God (Mark 3:5). He wept at the tomb of a dear friend (John 11:35), and as He faced the agony of the Cross, He was troubled within (John 12:27).

The Son of Man

Jesus calls Himself the Son of Man 80 times in the Gospels. Though He claimed attributes of Deity as Son of Man, He at the same time asserted His identification with *us* as sons of men. His humanity, in fact, was unique in that it was *complete*. Our Lord, as a man, was "free from both hereditary depravity and from actual sin, as is shown by His never offering sacrifice, never praying for [His own] forgiveness, teaching that all but He needed the new birth, challenging all to convict Him of a single sin."[17]

Christ's humanity was as real and genuine as His Deity. Both must be maintained and neither may be emphasized at the expense of the other.

Mostly Man or Mostly God?

A brief review of Church History will illustrate how easy it is to emphasize one aspect of Christ's nature over the other. Some of these tendencies are with us to this day and we must guard against them. Heresies forced the Early Church to define clearly her belief in the Deity and humanity of Christ. These definitions were not innovations, but merely crystallized what was already held to be biblical truth.

The Ebionites, early in the Second Century, denied the Deity of Christ. They maintained He was merely a man, though perhaps supernaturally conceived. They conceded that, though a man, He held a peculiar relationship to God, especially from the time of His baptism — when, they held, the fulness of the Holy Spirit rested on Him.

On the other hand, the Docetists, later in the same century, denied the true humanity of Jesus. They rejected the reality of His human body and suggested that it was merely a phantom and only

49

appeared to be human. This view was the logical conclusion of their assumption that matter is inherently evil. They implied that the divine Christ was not hungry and thirsty, nor did He suffer and die. Jesus' life on earth, they maintained, was largely an illusion.

The Arians, forerunners of today's Unitarians, mistook the biblical statements about Christ's subordination to the Father as teaching His inferiority. They taught that Christ was somehow created by the Father as the first and highest of created beings, but that He Himself was not eternally self-existent. This belief is current today in several major cults.

Another deviation was that of the Apollinarians, who were condemned at the Council of Constantinople in A.D. 381. Heavily influenced by Greek philosophy, Apollinarius taught that Christ had a true body and soul and that in Him the place of the human mind or spirit was taken by His divine being. If this were true, however, it would mean that Jesus was not fully human and therefore was not tried or tempted in every respect as we are.

In the Fifth Century, Nestorius so emphasized the distinctness of Christ's two natures that he denied the real union between the divine and human in our Lord. He made this union a moral one rather than an organic one. Nestorians virtually believed in two natures and two persons instead of two natures in one person.

The Eutychians, on the other hand, were on the opposite extreme, denying the distinction and coexistence of the two natures. They said that the divine and the human natures in Christ mingled into a third sort of nature, peculiar to Christ. They seemed to believe that Christ's human nature was really absorbed into His divine nature, though the divine nature was, by this "merger," somewhat changed from what it had been before the union. This group was condemned as heretical at the Council of Chalcedon in A.D. 451.

The question of the two natures of Christ is obviously complex, with numerous subtleties. The orthodox doctrine, promulgated at Chalcedon in 451, says that "in the one person, Jesus Christ, there are two natures, a human nature and a divine nature, each in its completeness and integrity, and that these two natures are organically and indissolubly united, yet so that no third nature is formed thereby. In brief, to use the antiquated dictum, orthodox doctrine forbids us either to divide the person or confound the natures."[18]

The Deity and humanity of Christ's one Person is admittedly a profound subject, and it raises many questions. This concept is similar to that of the Trinity — we know by revelation that it is true, but have no satisfactory explanation.

In an attempt to explain Christ's two natures, some have suggested various "kenosis" theories. The term *kenosis* comes from the Greek word for "emptied" (Phil. 2:7). Some have contended that Christ totally emptied Himself of Deity and was limited to the natural knowledge and ability of an ordinary man. Others have held that though He renounced His divine attributes, He still somehow possessed them. Still others have suggested that our Lord suspended His divine consciousness at His conception and reassumed it in manhood. Hammond comments that, "our Lord's attributes of Deity were at no time laid aside. Any 'explanation' of His divine-human nature which violates the integrity of His Deity is obviously to be rejected, and there seems to be no explanation that is without grave difficulties. The nearest we can get is that our Lord's perfect divine nature (with the possession of all its attributes) was so united with a perfect human nature that a single divine-human Personality developed with the divine element (if such a distinction can be made here) controlling the normal development of the human. Beyond this we cannot safely go."[19]

The Early Church creeds did not try to explain the mystery of how Christ's two natures were united in one Person. They recognized His full manhood and His true Deity, but they did not solve the problem of bringing the two modes of His self-manifestation — manhood and Deity — into the unity of a single person. From the beginning, it must have been obvious that the truth lay between two unacceptable tendencies — to break the Person into two, or to mingle the natures so that the result was neither truly human nor truly divine. In a statement which the Early Church found acceptable, and which has been used ever since, Athanasius said, "He became what He was not; He continued to be what He was." This is really a terse affirmation rather than an explanation.

In an effort to eliminate the difficulties that

arise from the problem of Christ's two natures, theologians — as we have seen — go to either of two extremes. Some exalt Christ's human nature to a level that would separate Him from the rest of humanity. For example, they say His nature was that of unfallen Adam. For this, there is no evidence in the Gospel records of His earthly life. Others, on the other hand, water down His Deity, defining the Incarnation as involving a *kenosis* or self-emptying, for which the word used in Philippians 2:7 gives no support. This view makes our Lord, on earth, subject to all human limitation — with, of course, the exception of sin.

"The factor that is forgotten, and may well be the only key to the problem, is the ministry of the Holy Spirit in the Person and life of Christ. That Spirit, who had prepared His humanity and kept the unborn Child free from the taint of a mother's sin, never left Him, but throughout all the temptations and sufferings of His life and death brought to His human soul the light and comfort and strength which He needed to accomplish His task. In the light of that gracious ministry, we can understand, in some measure, how the divine nature was acting under human conditions, and how the human nature was acting in the fullest unity with the divine. That Spirit, who shared the eternal counsels of the Godhead, unified the consciousness of Christ so that there could be no possibility of division or dualism within Him. For this reason we can understand how there was nothing unnatural or unhuman about the self-consciousness of Jesus, even when He was in unbroken communion with the supernatural and eternal.

"However we explain it — and a full knowledge passes our comprehension — saving faith has always reached out to One who is perfect man, true God, and one Christ, and in the strength and fellowship of this faith we as Christians are called to abide."[20]

A proper knowledge of Christ's Person is crucial in understanding His work. If He were not the God-man, His work could not have eternal and personal significance for us.

What Christ Did

We have already considered the claims of our Lord to Deity and the way He vindicated His claims by an authority over natural forces which could only have been supernatural. While fully appreciating who Jesus *is*, however, we must not overlook the equally important significance of what He has *done* — and is doing — for believers.

If Jesus were not fully God, He *could* not be our Saviour. But if He were God and yet did nothing on our behalf — that is, did not *do* something to bring us to God — He *would* not be our Saviour. Being God *qualified* Jesus Christ to be Saviour, but His atoning death for us *made* Him our Saviour. Jesus not only *could* save men; He *did*.

Christ was the perfect Man. As such, He was without sin in thought, word, or deed. He was able to challenge His enemies with the question, "Which of you convicts Me of sin?" (cf. John 8: 46, NAS). His foes had no reply. He was totally obedient to the Father. "My meat," He told His disciples, "is to do the will of Him that sent Me, and to finish His work" (John 4:34).

There are three reasons why our Lord's perfect life was a necessity.

1. It qualified Him to become the sacrificial offering for sin. Old Testament types all insist on the purity of the victim for sacrifice.

2. It meant that perfect obedience was rendered to God, in contrast to Adam's disobedience. Scripture emphasizes this repeatedly (Rom. 5:19; Heb. 10:6, 7).

3. By it He became a qualified Mediator and High Priest for His people (Heb. 2:11-18).[21]

Our Lord was, par excellence, "a Man with a mission." He frequently said, at a point of crisis, "Mine hour is *not yet* come" (John 2:4; cf. 7:6). Finally He said, "The hour *is come* that the Son of Man should be glorified" (John 12:23). A little later, as He contemplated the awfulness of the Cross, He said, "Now is My soul troubled; and what shall I say? Father, save Me from this hour. But for this cause came I unto this hour" (John 12:27). The reason He had come, as He had said, was to "seek and to save that which was lost" (Luke 19:10) and to "give His life a ransom for many" (Mark 10:45). So central is the death of Christ to an understanding of Christianity that we will discuss it more fully in a later chapter.

Christ Left the Grave

But not only did our Lord live and die. The triumphant dynamic of Christianity is that *He arose from the dead.* The common greeting of the Early Church was the dramatic reminder, "He is risen!" The thing that changed a handful of cowardly, frightened disciples, who denied that they even knew their leader (Matt. 26:56, 70, 72, 74), into roaring lions proclaiming the faith, was the fact that they had seen Jesus, alive from the dead. Peter declared in Jerusalem, at the risk of his life, and just 50 days after the Resurrection, "This Jesus hath God raised up, whereof we all are witnesses" (Acts 2:32). Both the death and the resurrection of Christ show His supremacy and His uniqueness among all the religious leaders of the world.

A number of times Jesus predicted both His death and His resurrection (Mark 8:31; 10:32-34; cf. Matt. 16:21, etc.). But such a statement was so fantastic that the disciples didn't believe it until, after his entombment, they had the firsthand evidence of seeing Him themselves.

It is important to understand that the resurrection of Christ was a *bodily* resurrection, not one of "spirit" or "influence," as is sometimes suggested. The disciples, on first seeing Jesus after He rose, thought they were seeing a ghost and were terribly frightened. Our Lord had to say to them, "Behold My hands and My feet, that it is I Myself: handle Me, and see; for a spirit hath not flesh and bones as ye see Me have" (Luke 24:39). He proceeded to eat fish and honey with them to further demonstrate His physical reality. He invited doubting Thomas to put his finger in the nail-prints and put his hand in the pierced side (John 20:27), so giving further testimony to the physical nature of His resurrection body and also indicating that this was the body that had been crucified and buried.

His risen body, however, differed from our bodies and from His own previous body. For instance, our risen Lord passed through closed doors when He met with the disciples for the first time in the Upper Room (John 20:19). Paul discusses at some length the subject of the Resurrection and the resurrection body (1 Cor. 15). This passage should be studied carefully.

Resurrection Implications

The implications of the Resurrection are enormous. We should understand them as fully as possible — and *enjoy* them.

First, as we have seen, the Resurrection fully confirms the truth and value of what Jesus taught and did. Paul says, "If Christ be not raised, your faith is vain; ye are yet in your sins" (1 Cor. 15:17). Because of the Resurrection, we know we are not trusting in a myth; we know that our sins are actually forgiven through the death of Christ. Certainty and forgiveness are based on the empty tomb! Christ is the only One who has ever come back from death to tell men about the beyond. In *His* words we know we have the authoritative Word of God Himself.

Second, Christ's resurrection is the guarantee of our own resurrection. Jesus said, "Because I live, ye shall live also" (John 14:19). We know with assurance that the grave is not our end, and that we shall be raised as He was.

Third, we know that the body is in itself good, not inherently evil, as some have mistakenly thought. The fact that our Lord became flesh and took a physical body in the Incarnation shows this. It is confirmed by the Resurrection, which tells us that in the eternal state, body and soul will be reunited, though the body will, of course, be a glorified body like our Lord's. Christ is the One "who shall change our vile [weak] body that it may be fashioned like unto His glorious body" (Phil. 3:21).

Fourth, we have assurance of the contemporary power of Christ in life today. We do not believe in a dead Christ hanging on a cross or lying in a grave, but in the risen Christ of the empty tomb. Christ gives us His life in salvation. This is the contemporary power, the dynamic, of Christian faith.

Many attempts have been made to explain away the Resurrection. A full discussion cannot be gone into here.

In summary, we can say that some false theories of the Resurrection (such as the swoon theory) revolve around denial of Christ's actual death. Other views hold that the disciples made an honest error which led them sincerely but wrongly to proclaim that Jesus had risen from the dead.

But all attempts to explain away the Resurrection founder on the rocks of the actual evidence. Christ would have been a deceiver had He only swooned and allowed the disciples to think He had actually risen from the dead. The disciples were not prepared for a hallucination. They didn't *expect* He *would* rise and they didn't *believe* He *had* risen from the dead. They had to be persuaded against their "better judgment" that it was so (Luke 24:36-45). Furthermore, Christ appeared ten different times, in different places, and in one case to more than 500 people at once. Such an event cannot be explained by "hallucination." The disciples would have been deceivers at best if they had stolen Christ's body. Nearly all of them died for their faith, however, in martyrdom. People will die for what they mistakenly *think* is true, but they don't die for what they *know* is false. The inability of the enemies of Christ to produce His body is further evidence that it had not been stolen.

The empty tomb, the revolutionized lives of the disciples, the Lord's Day (worship being shifted from Saturday to Sunday because of the Resurrection), the existence of the Christian Church (which can be traced back to approximately A.D. 30) — all are conclusive evidence that the Resurrection is fact, not fiction. The final evidence is the transformation of those today who have met and been given new life by the risen Christ.

Ascension, Exaltation

Jesus not only predicted His death and resurrection, but also His ascension and exaltation (John 6:62; 17:1). In the ascension, He visibly left His disciples and the earth and returned to heaven, 40 days after His resurrection. His exit from this life was as miraculous as His entrance. The account of it is given in Acts 1:9-11.

Christ having ascended, God the Father has given Him a place of exaltation in heaven. God has "set Him at His own right hand in the heavenly places, far above all principality and power and might and dominion, and every name that is named" (Eph. 1:20, 21). Christ has a position of power and glory. His ascension and exaltation were necessary for the completion of His work of redemption. As the ascended and exalted Christ, He has entered heaven as a forerunner for us (Heb. 6:20). We are to follow Him. He is able to enter into the heavenly counterpart of the holy of holies in the earthly tabernacle because of the merits of His atonement. Believers will be able to follow Him because the blood of His atonement has been applied to them.

Christ is now before God as our High Priest and Advocate. He appears "in the presence of God for us" (Heb. 9:24). "If any man sin, we have an Advocate with the Father, Jesus Christ the righteous" (1 John 2:1). As our Mediator, Christ is now active for us before the throne of God.

Christ has gone to prepare a place for us in heaven. He clearly told the disciples that He would do so and come again "and receive you unto Myself, that where I am, there ye may be also" (John 14:3, 4). Every Christian should look forward with deep anticipation to the return of his Lord for him.

Because of the ascension and exaltation of Christ, we have free and confident access into the very presence of God. We can "come boldly unto the throne of grace" (Heb. 4:16). In Old Testament times, access to the presence of God was limited to one person — the high priest; to one place — the holy of holies in the Tabernacle (or the Temple); and to one time — the Day of Atonement. But because Christ is our High Priest and has passed into the heavens, *each* of us has access to the Creator at *any* time and at *any* place. How the angels must wonder that we make so little use of this privilege of audience with the King!

Christianity is Christ from beginning to end. To know who Christ is and what He has done is to increase our awe, wonder, and appreciation of the One who, though He was rich, for our sakes became poor, that we through His poverty might be rich (2 Cor. 8:9).

For Further Reading

Anderson, J. N. D. *Evidence for the Resurrection.* Chicago: Inter-Varsity Press, 1966.

Berkouwer, G. C. *The Person of Christ.* Grand Rapids: Eerdmans, 1954.

Harrison, E. F. *A Short Life of Christ.* Grand Rapids: Eerdmans, 1968.

Little, Paul. *Know Why You Believe.* Wheaton, Ill.: Scripture Press, 1967.

Morris, Leon. *The Lord From Heaven.* London: Inter-Varsity Fellowship, 1958.

Warfield, B. B. *The Person and Work of Christ,* ed. S. G. Craig. Nutley, N.J.: Presbyterian and Reformed Publishing Co., 1950.

Chapter 4

Christ's Death

Christianity is Christ, and unless we understand the death of Christ, we cannot possibly appreciate why our Lord came into human history. Without the death of Christ, there could be no forgiveness of sins and hence no salvation. Jesus Himself said, "The Son of Man is come to seek and to save that which was lost" (Luke 19:10) and, "The Son of Man came not to be ministered to, but to minister, and to give His life a ransom for many" (Mark 10:45), clearly pointing to the redemptive nature of His death.

In the death of Christ we have another "uniqueness" of Christianity. Here God has done for man what man cannot do for himself. God provided a way by which man, who is sinful and corrupt, can be forgiven, cleansed, and brought into vital and intimate relationship with his Maker — not on the basis of something *man* must do, but on the basis of what God Himself, in His Son, has *done*.

Every other religious system in the world is essentially a "do-it-yourself" proposition. Only in Christianity is salvation a free gift, offered not because man deserves it but because of the incomprehensible goodness of God's love. The cross of Christ is the central fact of human history. Jesus was the only Man born to die (Heb. 2:14). His death is the basis for His personal worthiness to receive the worship of the whole creation (Rev. 5:9, 12, 13).

Christ's death is a central theme of the Scriptures, both Old Testament and New. As far back as the Garden of Eden, when God cursed the serpent, He promised the Deliverer (Gen. 3:15). The Prophet Isaiah gives us a clear promise of One who would die for our sins: "He was wounded for our transgressions; He was bruised for our iniquities; the chastisement of our peace was upon Him; and with His stripes we are healed. All we like sheep have gone astray; we have turned every one to his own way, and the Lord hath laid on Him the iniquity of us all" (Isa. 53:5, 6).

In order to explain the recent puzzling events in Jerusalem to the two disciples walking to Emmaus, Jesus showed them *all* the Scriptures pointing to His death (Luke 24:25-27). His conversation must have been one of the most exciting Bible studies of all time. His death was a subject about which the prophets wrote much. They spoke of His sufferings without knowing exactly who He was or when He would come. They were told they were writing for the benefit of others than themselves (1 Peter 1:10-12).

Some question the necessity for *understanding* the meaning of the Cross and the Atonement. After all, they argue, we are not saved by any theory of the Atonement, but by the actual death of Christ. This, of course, is true. We must be careful not to try to reduce the Atonement into merely a neat formula. On the other hand, just as what we believe about Christ's person is crucial — even though we are saved by what He has *done* — so it is important for us to understand the meaning of His mission to die for man's sin. Otherwise we may find ourselves wittingly or unwittingly opposing the Gospel in one of its most vital and fundamental teachings.

Old Testament Background

A clear understanding of the significance of the death of Christ requires an understanding of the Old Testament background which led up to it.

Man is hopelessly separated from God because of His sin: "But your iniquities have separated between you and your God, and your sins have hid His face from you, that He will not hear" (Isa. 59:2). God takes the initiative and provides the way by which our estrangement may be ended. Leon Morris comments, "In the Old Testament, [atonement] is usually said to be obtained by the sacrifices, but it must never be forgotten that God says of the atoning blood, 'I have given it to you upon the altar to make an atonement for your souls' (Lev. 17:11). Atonement is secured not by any value inherent in the sacrificial victim, but because sacrifice is the divinely appointed way of securing atonement."[22]

The whole sacrificial system of the Old Testament was a symbolic portrayal of what would be completely fulfilled in Christ. The Passover, celebrated at the time of the Exodus of the Israelites from Egypt, is the fullest picture. Each believing family slew a perfect lamb and put its blood on the doorposts and lintels of the house. The angel of death, when he saw the blood, passed over that household, which in this way escaped the judgment of having its firstborn die. As with other sacrifices, the elements of perfection, the shedding of blood, and substitution were all present.

Christ was the fulfillment of all that the Passover lamb stood for. He was "the Lamb of God which taketh away the sin of the world" (John 1:29). Those who in faith offered animal sacrifices in Old Testament times looked forward to the coming Messiah, just as we by faith look back to the cross of Christ. The animal sacrifices did not save, but faith in what they symbolized *did*. We by faith lay hold on the fulfillment of the symbols.

> Not all the blood of beasts
> On Jewish altars slain,
> Could give the guilty conscience peace,
> Or wash away the stain.
> But Christ the heavenly Lamb,
> Takes all our sins away;
> A sacrifice of nobler name
> And richer blood than they.

Atonement for Sin

Christ's death is spoken of as the atonement for our sin. It has been suggested that "atonement" means, basically, "at-one-ment" — that is to say, a bringing together of those who are estranged. But the Old Testament word means, essentially, "to cover." The animal sacrifices provided a "covering" for sin until the death of Christ would put it forever away.

In the New Testament, various ideas are presented which explain and illustrate Atonement. It is spoken of as a reconciliation: "When we were enemies, we were reconciled to God by the death of His Son" (Rom. 5:10, cf. 2 Cor. 5:18, 19; Eph. 2:16; and Col. 1:20). Reconciliation implies former hostility between the reconciled parties. As sinners, we were enemies of God. God, because of His holy character, is opposed to that which is sinful and unholy. The death of Christ did away with the cause of God's enmity by taking away our sin. We have been reconciled to God, the root cause of alienation having been removed and our attitude toward God having been changed. God has always loved us, and still loves us. But His wrath — the fixed, permanent attitude of God's holiness against evil — has been turned away from us. It has been carried by Christ.

The death of Christ is also spoken of as a propitiation: "God hath set [Him] forth to be a propitiation through faith in His blood, to declare His righteousness for the remission of sins that were past, through the forebearance of God" (Rom. 3:

25). Propitiation has within it the concept of "the removing of wrath by the offering of a gift."[23] It has a personal quality to it. A young man might propitiate his girlfriend, for example, by sending her a bouquet of roses. God, in this case, is propitiated because the perfect sacrifice of Christ, in laying down His life for us, has fully met the holy and just requirements of God's law.

It is important to understand that God does not first reconcile us and then love us. Rather, *because* God has loved us, He reconciles us and opens the way for propitiation.

"Ransom" is another term used to define the death of Christ. It is closely linked with the idea of redemption. "[Christ] gave Himself a ransom for all, to be testified in due time" (1 Tim. 2:6; cf. 1 Peter 1:18). Though some Church leaders seem to have thought this ransom was paid to Satan, the general conviction has been that it is the price paid to meet the holy requirements of God's law and redeem us from its curse. "Ye know that ye were not redeemed with corruptible things, as silver and gold . . . but with the precious blood of Christ, as a Lamb without blemish and without spot" (1 Peter 1:18, 19).

Our Substitute

Among the terms that give the clearest explanations of the death of Christ is "substitute." "Christ also hath once suffered for sins, the just for the unjust, that He might bring us to God" (1 Peter 3:18). Christ died *for* us — that is, in our place.

67

"[God] hath made Him who knew no sin to be sin for us, that we might be made the righteousness of God in Him" (cf. 2 Cor. 5:21). The whole concept of sacrifice for sin carries with it the idea of substitution, which is fulfilled in Christ, "who His own self bore our sins in His own body on the tree, that we, being dead to sins, should live unto righteousness; by whose stripes we are healed" (1 Peter 2:24).

In the doctrinal statements of many Bible-believing churches and institutions, specific and particular mention is made of the "substitutionary" atonement of Christ. The reason for this is that other interpretations of the atonement have been advanced which, though some of them contain partial truth, have tended to eclipse, if not deny outright, the central truth of substitutionary atonement. Some theologians openly attack this doctrine, suggesting that the idea of substitution is a Pauline addition to the teaching of Christ. Even from the small portion of Scripture we have examined, however, it is clear that such claims are not the case. The teaching that Christ has taken our place and suffered and died in our behalf is as present in the Gospels as in the rest of the New Testament.

Often the viewpoint of a speaker, minister, or author on the substitutionary atonement is a reliable indicator of the orthodoxy of his other theological views.

Among the many perverted views of the atonement are the following:

1. The *moral influence* or *example* theory. The

idea here is that man needs only to repent and reform to be reconciled to God. Advocates of this view believe the death of Christ is merely the powerful example of a man committed to truth and righteousness at all costs, and that we are redeemed as we allow His example to have a determining influence on our own efforts at moral improvement.

There is, of course, great moral influence in Christ's example. It is true that "Christ also suffered for us, leaving us an example that ye should follow in His steps" (1 Peter 1:21). But Scripture clearly teaches not only that sin has defiled us personally, but that because of it we are guilty before a holy God. Many passages of Scripture clearly teach that Christ died *for our sins,* and the moral influence theory ignores these passages entirely.

Other Erroneous Views

2. The *governmental* theory holds that the Atonement is a requirement of God's government of the universe, which "cannot be maintained, nor can the divine law preserve its authority over its subjects, unless the pardon of the offenders is accompanied by some exhibition of the high estimate which God sets upon His law and on the heinous guilt of violating it."[24] But why is *Christ* necessary, if this is all there is to the Atonement? And why should One who is *perfect* suffer, rather than one who is *guilty?*

It is true that the Cross shows man, with extreme vividness, the awfulness of sin, and that it is eloquent testimony that man may not ignore or toy with the law of God. But this surely is incidental to Christ's being made sin for us so that we may be made the righteousness of God in Him (2 Cor. 5:21). This view also fails to do justice to all the passages of Scripture already referred to.

3. Some have felt that the crucifixion of Christ was simply an untimely *accident of history*, unexpected and unforeseen. But Scripture clearly contradicts this view. Christ Himself assured His disciples that it was for this purpose that He had come into the world (John 12:27). In the Garden of Gethsemane He prayed to His heavenly Father, "Nevertheless, not as I will but as Thou wilt" (Matt. 26:39). He says further, "Therefore doth My Father love Me, because I lay down My life, that I may take it again. No man taketh it from Me, but I lay it down of Myself. I have power to lay it down, and I have power to take it again" (John 10:17, 18). The prophets predicted the Messiah's sacrificial death and, in fact, all scriptural evidence opposes the idea that Christ's death was accidental. That Christ did not *have* to die, but voluntarily endured the Cross for us, is one of the central and most moving aspects of His sacrifice.

4. Others would suggest that though Christ's death might have been anticipated by sensitivity to the gathering storm, He died, essentially, as *another martyr* of history. But if this were the case, how could forgiveness come from His death, and how do we account for Jesus' statement, when He

began the ceremony we celebrate as the Lord's Supper, "This is My blood of the New Testament, which is shed for many for the remission of sins" (Matt. 26:28)? The whole emphasis of the Scripture is opposed to any view of the Cross that is less than supernatural.

The idea of substitution is a basic theme throughout the Bible. There are other lessons to be learned from the Atonement, to be sure, but none is so prominent as to obscure this basic and wonderful truth.

Objections to Substitution

There have always been objections to the substitutionary atonement, and we should consider some of them.

Some insist that if God does not pardon sin without requiring atonement, He must either not be all-powerful or else not be a God of love. "Why can't He simply forgive sin out of His pure mercy?" skeptics want to know. "Could not an all-powerful God, in His omnipotence, have redeemed the world as easily as He created it? Since God commands man to forgive freely, why does He Himself not freely forgive?"

Finlayson summarizes the answer given such questions by Anselm in the Twelfth Century: God cannot so forgive because He is not a private person, but God. God's will is not His own in the sense that anything is permissible to Him or becomes right because He wills it. What God determines is what God does. God cannot deal with

71

sin except as in His holiness He sees it to be. If He did not punish it, or make adequate satisfaction for it, then He would be forgiving it unjustly.[25]

It is important to realize, as we have previously pointed out, that God exercises all His attributes in harmony with each other. His holiness demands atonement for sin. His love provides it. God's attributes never violate one another, nor are they antagonistic to each other. They are not in an uneasy equilibrium, but they work together in full and complete harmony. "Mercy is shown not by trampling upon the claims of justice, but by vicariously satisfying them."[26] In the cross of Christ, "Mercy and truth are met together: righteousness and peace have kissed each other" (Ps. 85:10).

Love and Holiness

The New Testament speaks of the "wedding," or coming together, of the attributes of God's love and holiness in the cross of Christ so that "He might be just and the justifier of him which believeth in Jesus" (Rom. 3:26). In the very act of forgiving sin, or, to use Paul's "daring word . . . of 'justifying the ungodly,' God must act in harmony with His whole character. He must show what He is in relation to sin — that evil cannot dwell with Him because He refuses to tolerate sin in any form. In the very process of making forgiveness available to men, He must show His complete abhorrence of sin. In other words, God must not merely forgive men, but must forgive in a way which shows that He forever hates evil and can never treat it as other than completely hateful. Sin makes a real difference to God, and even in forgiving, He cannot ignore sin or regard it as other or less than it is. If He did so, He would not be more gracious than He is in the Atonement — He would cease to be God."[27]

Others have said that the very idea of God's permitting *Christ* to die for *our* sin, as an innocent victim for guilty sinners, was injustice rather than justice. Some go so far as actually to call it immoral. But such charges would be true only if Christ were an unwilling victim. As we have seen, the glory of the Cross is in the *voluntary* nature of Christ's coming to earth. "He did not consider equality with God a thing to be grasped, but humbled Himself and became obedient to death, even the death of the cross" (cf. Phil. 2: 6-8). Hammond observes, "The Sufferer must have a double connection between God and Himself on the one hand, and the sinner and Himself on the other."[28] Only a solidly scriptural objection could fairly be raised against evangelical teaching on this subject.

Though we must consider alternative interpretations, we must note that critics approach the doctrine of substitution from their preconceived notions of what God *ought to have done* and their own superficial and humanistic ethical standards.

Other Questions

In addition to the objections we have already mentioned, certain other questions may come to your mind about the substitutionary death of Christ. How, for example, could the death of one Person atone for the innumerable sins of the whole world?

At the human level, such atonement would obviously be impossible. One person may die for one other, but for no more than one other. But when we consider the effectiveness of the death of Christ, we must remember who died. Christ was not merely a man; He was the God-man: "God was in Christ" (2 Cor. 5:19). Christ's life was of infinite value, and His death likewise had infinite worth. The sum total of the value of all of those for whom He died does not approximate the infinite value of the divine life that was given at Calvary in sacrifice for our sakes.

In the "value" of the One who died is also the answer to the question, "Since Christ was only dead for three days, how can His experience be compared with the eternal death millions will experience if they do not trust Him?" The death Christ died was an infinite death, both in value and in the intensity of the spiritual suffering the Son of God went through. We simply cannot comprehend what it must have been for the sinless Son of God to become sin (2 Cor. 5:21) for us.

There is also the question as to whether, when Christ died, it is true to say that "*God* died." Robert J. Little points out, in answer to this question, that Christ "became a man in order to die, for without dying as a man He could not have delivered men from the penalty of sin. . . . Yet when He died, His *divine being* did not die. And when He died as a man, it was only His body which died. Scripture makes it clear that when *any* human being dies, it is the body which dies. The soul and spirit live on. Hence, when Christ died, we do not say that God died, though He who died on the cross was God. No finite mind can fully understand everything about the infinite God, but we can have some understanding of what is involved."[29]

A number of clear implications arise out of an understanding of the Atonement.

One is that in the Atonement we are dealing with an absolute issue of life and death. The Bible clearly tells us that "the wages of sin is death, but the gift of God is eternal life through Jesus Christ our Lord" (Rom. 6:23). Some tend to hedge on drawing lines between those who are saved and those who are lost. This hedging is perhaps due to their reluctance to judge individuals and perhaps also because of their incipient hope that all are saved.

It is true that only the Lord knows those who are His, and that our judgment, based on a man's profession in words and on the external nature of his life, may be faulty. But the Scripture knows no such vagueness. "He that believeth on the Son *hath everlasting life;* and he that believeth not the Son *shall not see life,* but the wrath of God *abideth* on him" (John 3:36). Men are in sin and Christ died for their sin. A man is *now* either in Christ by faith, or still in sin because of unbelief. There is no in-between ground. A person has either life or death, lives either in light or in darkness, is either saved or lost.

Other Implications

It is in the death of Christ that we can see clearly why some widespread ideas of the universal Fatherhood of God are erroneous. Often accompanying a reluctance to draw distinctions, people who hold these ideas suggest that all men are God's children and that therefore efforts to "convert" them are in bad taste. But though we all *are* God's offspring by creation (Acts 17:28), we are not God's children spiritually, else the Atonement would have been unnecessary. Jesus spoke sharply to those who refused to recognize Him as God, saying, "Ye are of your father the devil" (John 8:44). On the other hand, "to all who did accept Him, and trust in His name, He gave the right *to become* the children of God" (John 1:12, wms). We cannot *become* what we already *are*.

The death of Christ is what makes the Gospel good *news* rather than good *advice*. Christ did not die for us because we recognized our need and cried out to God for help. "But God proves His own love for us by Christ's dying for us when we were still sinners" (Rom. 5:8, berk). The Gospel is not a set of swimming instructions for a drowning man, but a pardon and reprieve from death for a man who does not deserve it. There is nothing we must or can *do* to benefit from it, except simply to receive it as a free gift and so experience eternal life.

Basis for Assurance

The Atonement is what gives a Christian his basis for assurance of forgiveness of sin and eternity in heaven. This assurance is not arrogant presumption that *we* are better than anyone else, but rather confidence, based on God's own Word, in what Christ has done for us by dying on the cross. From the cross, just before He died, Jesus said, "It is finished" (John 19:30). So we speak of the *"finished work of Christ."* By this we mean that our Lord has already done everything necessary for our salvation. We still need daily cleansing and forgiveness of sin, of course, and we receive it when we confess our sin (1 John 1:9). But we receive forgiveness on the basis of what has already been accomplished in us — as sons, not as alienated sinners. God intends us to have assurance of our salvation: "These things have I written to you that believe on the name of the Son of God, *that ye may know* that ye have eternal life" (1 John 5:13).

Assurance need not lead to indifference and smug contentment, as many contend it does. It can also result in deep joy and a loving response to Christ because of His love for us. We are continually reminded, "Ye are not your own . . . ye are bought with a price; therefore glorify God in your body and in your spirit, which are God's" (1 Cor. 6:19, 20). The new life we receive changes our attitudes, motives, values, and will. In ourselves we are incapable of such changes, but in Christ we become new creations (2 Cor. 5:17). It is for this reason that Paul was so daring and so adamant in maintaining that the Church add nothing to simple trust as a requirement for salvation, and add nothing afterward by way of legal regulation to maintain salvation. The Gospel is not Christ "plus" something, however good the something may be, but Christ *alone* in His atoning death for us.

Demonstrates God's Love

The Atonement also demonstrates the nature and character of God's love. We live in a world which is acutely aware of man's pain, suffering, and misery. No one is interested in a God who is aloof and untouched by human need, or even in a God who might save sinners from a distance. In the cross of Christ the affirmation, "God is love," takes concrete expression. People will believe a demonstration of love in action before they will believe a person who declares it only in words. God's love for us is no exception. John says, "Hereby perceive we the love of God, because He laid down His life for us" (1 John 3:16).

God, in Christ, became involved in this life. He assumed its burdens and entered into its tragedies. Finally He took on full responsibility for this life by "becoming sin for us . . . that we might be made the righteousness of God in Him" (cf. 2 Cor. 5:21). Through the Atonement, we know dramatically that God is not indifferent to man's tragedy and suffering.

The death of Christ, in its objective accom

plishment and in its subjective impact, is the central fact of history.

> Love so amazing, so divine
> Demands my soul, my life, my all.

For Further Reading

James Denney. *The Death of Christ*. Chicago: Inter Varsity Fellowship, 1964.

Guillebaud, H. E. *Why the Cross*. London: Inter-Varsity Fellowship, 1967.

Morris, Leon. *The Apostolic Preaching of the Cross*. London: Tyndale Press, 1965.

_____. *The Cross in the New Testament*. Grand Rapids: Eerdmans, 1964.

Chapter 5

Man and Sin

"What is man?" asked the psalmist David, centuries ago. It is striking that this is also the burning question of the 20th Century and the Space Age. Is man merely a glorified animal? Is he merely the sum total of all his chemicals and their reactions? Or is he more than this?

As the genetic code is deciphered and the electronic aspects of the brain's functioning are understood, the problem becomes increasingly urgent.

"Who am I?" The piercing question of identity must be answered by every person. Our answer, whether we realize it or not, has enormous influence upon our thinking and acting, our outlook, and our living. Never was it more important for a Christian to understand what the Bible says about man in order to have an anchor on the sea of human speculation.

The first question to be answered is that of man's origin. Where did he come from? "In the

beginning God created the heaven and the earth"
(Gen. 1:1), says the Bible, and, "God said, 'Let
Us make man in Our image, after Our likeness; and
let them have dominion over the fish of the sea,
and over the fowl of the air, and over the cattle,
and over all the earth, and over every creeping
thing that creepeth upon the earth.' So God created man is His own image, in the image of God
created He him; male and female created He them"
(vv. 26, 27).

Scripture consistently teaches that neither the
universe nor man himself is the product of blind
chance. Man, especially, is the result of careful
and purposeful deliberation on the part of the
members of the triune Godhead.

Adam, the first man, was created in God's image.
Adam is a proper name, but the Hebrew term
from which it comes also has the connotation of
"mankind." It is frequently so used in the Old
Testament.

God said, "It is not good that the man should
be alone," and to complement man He made a
woman to be Adam's helper (Gen. 2:18, 22).

"Through faith we understand that the worlds
[universe] were framed by the Word of God, so
that things which are seen were not made of things
which do appear" (Heb. 11:3). In other words,
God created matter *ex nihilo* (out of nothing). He
then formed matter into inanimate objects — plants,
animals, and man.

The Bible does not claim to tell us *how* man
and the universe were created. It does, however,
assert emphatically and unambiguously *that God*

81

brought them into being. Nowhere does the Bible attempt to *prove* God. It *assumes* Him. A Christian unashamedly begins with the assumption that God exists. He is convinced that the life, death, and resurrection of Christ clearly bear out this assumption. Such assumption is not naive or un-intellectual, and we should keep in mind that un-believers who reject the biblical view of Creation also begin with presuppositions and assumptions on which they base *their* claims. *Everyone* begins somewhere with an assumption that is not provable in the scientific sense. For a helpful, brief, contemporary discussion of the issues involved, see *The Creation of Matter, Life, and Man,* by Addison H. Leitch.

It is also important to realize that New Testament writers saw Adam as a person as historical as our Lord Himself. Paul clearly considered Adam to be a distinct individual as well as the prototype of fallen man (Rom. 5:12-21; 1 Cor. 15:22). Our Lord spoke about the creation of man, confirming the Genesis account (Matt. 19:4). There is no room for mythical or allegorical interpretations of the historicity of Adam's creation and subsequent fall.

Man was distinct and unique from the rest of creation. He was to subdue it and have dominion over it. He is at the top of all living beings. Man's self-consciousness, his capacity for intelligent reasoning, and, above all, his moral and spiritual sense, set him completely apart from all other creatures. No creature other than man has ever been observed building a chapel.

Body, Soul, and Spirit

Genesis 2 gives further information on the creation of man: "And the Lord God formed man of the dust of the ground and breathed into his nostrils the breath of life; and man became a living soul" (v. 7). It is clear that two elements were involved in man's creation. One is "the dust of the ground." The other is "the breath of life," which was given by God. The union of these two elements makes man a living being.

Man is clearly more than one substance. But are the components of his being *three* (body, soul, and spirit) or *two* (body and soul)? The Old Testament does not have a fixed term for the immaterial part of man's nature. The terms "soul," "heart," and "spirit" are used as counterparts of the material side. Along with the term "body," they include the whole man. The psalmist says, "My *soul* thirsteth for Thee, my *flesh* longeth for Thee" (63:1). But not all such biblical expressions indicate a twofold nature of man. Others just as plainly speak of *three* aspects of man's being: "My *soul* longeth . . . for the courts of the Lord: my *heart* and my *flesh* crieth out for the living God" (Ps. 84:2).

Should the God-breathed part of man be viewed as *two* parts — i.e., *soul* and *spirit* separately — or as *one?* Hammond observes, " 'Soul' and 'spirit' are certainly not to be regarded as synonymous in scriptural language. But, on the other hand, they are not kept invariably distinct. Compare Psalm 74:19 with Ecclesiastes 3:21; Matthew 10:28 with

Luke 23:46; Acts 2:27 with 7:59. The references invoked in suggesting [threefold] division are those of 1 Thessalonians 5:23; Hebrews 4:12; cf. Luke 1:46, 47. . . . But those who suggest [such a division] admit that soul and spirit, in the body, are separable only in thought. It would seem best to regard them as differing aspects of the same essence, and to remember that whatever distinctions are made for the spiritual purposes of scriptural teaching, there is a substratum which is common to both soul and spirit."[30]

Man a Unity

In any case, the Bible always views man as a unity, both material and immaterial. The Resurrection shows that man is as essentially body as he is essentially soul or spirit. The notion that man is a soul imprisoned in a body is a Greek concept, not a biblical one.

What does it mean that man was created in the image and likeness of God? It certainly does not mean that he has any *physical* likeness to God. Scripture clearly teaches that God is a Spirit and does not have physical parts like a man (John 4:24). The Bible uses anthropomorphic expressions, such as "the hand of God," only to accommodate our human incapacity to think in any other terms. The strong prohibition against man's representing God by graven images was given because no one had ever seen God and therefore could not know how He looked. Nothing on earth *could* represent Him (Deut. 4:15-23; Ex. 20:4).

The image of God in man has to do, rather, with *personality*. Man has "a free, self-conscious, rational and moral personality like that of God — a nature capable of distinguishing right and wrong, of choosing the right and rejecting the wrong, and of ascending to the heights of spiritual attainment and communion with God."[31]

The original man was intelligent. He could give names to all the animals when they were presented to him (Gen. 2:19, 20). He had the power of reasoning and thought. In speaking, he could connect words and ideas. He had moral and spiritual qualities. He could and did commune with God and had the power to resist moral evil or yield to it (Gen. 3).

Because man has been created in the image of God, human life is inviolate. God instituted capital punishment (Gen. 9:6) for this reason.

The new man is *renewed* in the image of God in righteousness (Eph. 4:23, 24; Col. 3:10). The implication of "renewed" is that man once had a moral likeness to God, but that it was lost. Originally man was holy and the basic inclination of his nature was toward God. He was not *neutral* toward God, for the creation of the "new man" is after the pattern of the original. Nevertheless, from the beginning man had freedom to choose evil, and so to sin.

At the same time it is important to realize that man was also free *not* to sin. He had no original inward tendency to sin, as we have. Though he was capable of being tempted, he was not either *compelled* or *impelled* to sin. Adam *chose* to do so deliberately, as a free act. In the words of the famous phrase, man did not have inability to sin; he had ability *not* to sin.

Image vs. Likeness

Roman Catholics and some others distinguish between "image" and "likeness" because both words are used in Genesis 1:26. They have suggested that the *image* of God in man is only in his personality, and that the *likeness* of God is a supernatural gift given man by God in creation — i.e., "an original righteousness and perfect self-determination before God which could be, and indeed was, lost in the Fall. The *image*, on the other hand, consists of what belongs to man by nature, i.e., his free will, rational nature, and dominion over the animal world, which could not be lost even in the Fall. This would mean that the Fall destroyed what was originally supernatural in man, but left his nature and the image of God in him wounded, and his will free."[32]

This distinction, however, is not borne out by Scripture. The word "image" is used alone in Genesis 1:27 to describe what is meant by the two terms together in verse 26. In a similar construction elsewhere (Gen. 5:1), the word "likeness" is used alone.

Had things remained as they were in the original creation, all would have been well. Sin and death, with all their disastrous consequences for the human race, would never have come into being if Adam and Eve had chosen to obey rather than disobey by asserting their wills against God. But they *did* assert themselves against God, and their rebellion brought titanic disaster to all their descendants.

It is significant and intensely interesting that most, if not all, primitive religious traditions have, in one form or another, a belief in such a cataclysmic event. The Fall permanently altered what previously was an idyllic relationship between God and man. Man is generally viewed as having intimate fellowship with his Creator. But ever since he offended Him he has suffered from God's displeasure as well as from the loss of fellowship that resulted from his estrangement. Even in primitive animistic societies, which worship many gods, there is belief in a high-sky God who is the Creator. Since the passing of the golden age of intimate contact, this God is aloof from man. He now deals with human beings only through the lesser gods. All of these ideas seem to be echoes and reflections — distorted, faint, or mutilated by the passage of time — of the event, clearly described in the Bible (Gen. 3), which we call the Fall.

Personal Responsibility

The sin of Adam and Eve, as we have seen, was something for which they were personally responsible. They did not have sinful natures such as we have, so the temptation to sin must have come from outside them. The Bible describes this source as "the serpent" (Gen. 3:1), a term scripturally identified with Satan (Rev. 12:9). The Fall really explains how sin entered the human race, rather than how evil got into the world.

The ultimate answer to the profound question of the origin of evil is wrapped in the mysteries of God's counsels. Why did God not prevent evil from entering the universe, since He knew in advance what would happen? Why did He not make man incapable of sinning? He *could* have, but had He done so, we would not be human beings with freedom of choice. We would be robots, or "chatty dolls" that always speak the same word when someone pulls the string.

Though we have no final answers to sin's origin, God knew what would happen and, as someone has said, "thought it was worth the risk." C. S. Lewis observes that it is useless to speculate endlessly about the *origin* of evil. Each of us, however, faces the *fact* of evil, and the whole of God's redemptive program has to do with combatting it. God is not the Author of sin. Had our first parents not disobeyed Him, sin would never have entered the human race.

The several facets of sin are clear in the progression which is described in Genesis 3. Adam and Eve are first tempted to *doubt* God's Word ("Yea, hath God said?"), then led on to *disbelieve* it ("Ye shall not surely die"), and finally to *disobey* it ("They did eat").

The results of man's disobedience were immediate and obvious — separation from God and awareness of guilt. The curse which God pronounced involved, for mankind, both physical and spiritual death, hard physical labor, and sorrow. Man's fall involved the whole natural creation as well (cf. Rom. 8:21, 22).

As a result of the Fall, the image of God in man was badly marred in both its moral and its natural dimensions. Man lost his original inclination toward God and became a perverted creature, inclined away from his Creator. His personality was sadly marred. His intellect became bound, his emotions corrupted, and his will enslaved. He lost his true manhood. Men speak about man as "evolving" from a primitive condition, but the Bible (Rom. 1:18-32) graphically portrays his *descent* rather than *ascent.*

"Total Depravity"

The result was "total depravity." This expression of man's condition after the Fall has been widely misunderstood, with the result that the Christian position regarding man's sinful nature has sometimes been unjustly caricatured. The doctrine of depravity "was never intended to convey the meaning that man is as bad as he possibly can be and that every trace of moral rectitude has been lost in fallen man. 'Total depravity' is intended to indicate that the evil principle . . . has invaded each part of human nature, that there is no part of it which can now invariably perform righteous acts or invariably think righteous thoughts."[33] In other words, man's total depravity means that *every area of his life* is blighted — not that everything about

89

him is *totally bad.* His depravity is also total in that apart from God's grace he is forever lost.

The tragedy of the Fall went far beyond Adam and Eve. It was race-wide in its effect: "Wherefore as by one man sin entered into the world, and death by sin, . . . death passed upon all men, for all have sinned" (Rom. 5:12).

Men have held to three kinds of appraisals of the effect of the Fall on the human race:

1. The British monk, Pelagius, said that all men could be sinless if they chose, and that some men have lived free from sin. Pelagius reasoned that since a man can live free from sin, he must have been born into the world free from sin. Consequently, Adam's sin must have affected only Adam. In other words, Pelagius denied "original sin." Carrying his line of thinking further, he asserted that man has no need of supernatural help to live a righteous life. Pelagius did, however, recognize sin's force of habit and its harmful example to others.

2. Augustine, the great bishop of North Africa, rose to do battle with Pelagius' heretical view, and it is with his name that the *second* view of the Fall is connected. Augustine insisted that Adam transmitted to his posterity, because of the unity of the human race, both his guilt and the corruption belonging to it. The nature that man now has, said Augustine, is like the corrupted nature of Adam. Man has lost his freedom not to sin. He is free to carry out the desires of his nature — but since his nature itself is corrupt, he is really free only to do evil. Augustine used the phrase "the

will is free, but not freed." Though he has a free choice, man *chooses* a perverse course.

3. Roman Catholics hold a halfway position, called semi-Pelagianism — that in the Fall man lost the supernatural gift of righteousness which was not his by nature anyway, but had been added by God. In the Fall, man reverted to his natural state, without this righteousness that God had given him. So he is only *half* sick. Man, according to this view, still has a special gift of the Spirit which is sufficient to enable him to be righteous if he allows his will to cooperate with God's Spirit.

The Scripture is clear that though there may be a difference between men in their *degree* of sin, there is no difference in the *fact* of sin (cf. Rom. 3:9, 10, 22, 23; Isa. 53:6). The whole world is under judgment (Rom. 3:19), and because all men are apart from Christ, they are rebels against God, "children of disobedience," subject to His wrath (Eph. 2:2-4).

History and experience bear testimony to the universality of sin. The Augustinian view is closest to the biblical view — that man inherits a tendency to sin which always, to some extent, makes itself manifest. "And God saw that the wickedness of man was great in the earth and that every imagination of the thoughts of his heart was only evil continually. . . . The imagination of man's heart is evil from his youth" (Gen. 6:5; 8:21). When David said, "Behold, I was shapen in iniquity, and in sin did my mother conceive me" (Ps. 51:5), he was not speaking of the act of conception as sinful, but of the inherited bias to sin that is transmitted at conception.

Anyone who has ever had children recognizes clearly that self-centeredness shows up in the next generation at a very early age. You don't have to teach a child to be selfish. A great deal of effort, on the part of Christian parents, goes toward trying to overcome this tendency. The only one who has ever escaped this inherited bias toward sin is our Lord Himself.

Adam Our Representative

The Bible clearly teaches that Adam was our representative when he sinned (Rom. 5:12-19). Adam represented us just as, when our government declares war, it represents, affects, and involves us. As a result of Adam's sin, all who are in Adam die. This includes each of us. We tend to think that things might have turned out differently if we had been in Adam's place. But each of us, by doing as Adam did, has ratified the decision our first parents made to rebel and disobey God. Who would claim he had never sinned? And so we are justly condemned today not only for Adam's sin, but for our own sins.

But believers are also represented in Christ. The Bible teaches that as in Adam all die, so in Him all (believers) will be made alive (Rom. 5:19). The glory of the Gospel is that God did something for us in Christ that we could not do for ourselves. Because Adam's original sin is charged to us, we inherit a corrupt nature. Through Christ, the second Adam, we inherit a *new* nature. From Adam we received sin and guilt. From Christ we receive forgiveness and righteousness.

Sin, it is important to realize, does not begin with overt acts, nor is it limited to them. The acts proceed out of a corrupt heart and mind. In other words, we are not sinners because we sin — we sin because we are sinners. An apple tree is not an apple tree because it bears apples; it bears apples because it has the nature of an apple tree. Sins are the acts (or the apples); sin in our corrupt nature (the nature of the apple tree).

Through Christ we are not only forgiven our individual acts of sin, but we receive a new nature. The Gospel solution is radical, not merely one of outward reform. Someone has said, "Christ puts a new man in the suit — not just a new suit on the man." When the man himself is changed, his clothing (his particular actions) will tend to change as well.

Why We Are Responsible

But how can we be responsible for being sinners if God gave us a hopeless start in life? How can He then condemn us? The answer is twofold. First, as we have seen, we share Adam's sin. But beyond that, God has made full provision, through the sacrifice of Christ, for us to escape judgment. Scripture emphasizes man's ability to receive Christ if he wants to. As Jesus told Nicodemus, "*This* is the judgment: that light is come into the world, and man loved darkness rather than light" (cf. John

3:19). It has been said that the entrance to hell is guarded by a cross. No one comes into hell without walking past it. In other words, at Calvary God did everything necessary to keep man from judgment. If he refuses God's provision, man must himself bear responsibility for judgment.

But isn't it true, many people ask, that men are not all equally bad? Of course this is true. That "all have sinned" does not imply that all are as bad as they might be. But in relation to God's standard of holiness, all come short. You probably know honest, kind, and upright people who are not to be compared with the derelicts of Skid Row or with vicious criminals behind bars. Humanly, there are great differences.

But suppose we were to put one person in Death Valley, 280 feet below sea level; one in Denver, the mile-high city; and one on the peak of Mount Everest, altitude 29,000 feet. Let's suppose that the person in Death Valley represents the dregs of society and the kind of life such people live. The person in Denver is the "average man," and the one on Mount Everest is the best person you can imagine. The enormous differences in their altitude, or elevation, are apparent. But let's suppose God's standard of holiness is represented by the distance to the moon. Recently we have had an opportunity to see how Mount Everest, Denver, and Death Valley look from the moon. They're all the same!

From our human standpoint, there are great differences in men's sinfulness, but — contrasted with the infinite holiness of God — all men are equally lost.

Sin Is Against God

Sin is always primarily directed against God. It is more than mere self-centeredness. David, though he had wronged Bathsheba in adultery, and had murdered Uriah, cried out, "Against Thee, *Thee only*, have I sinned, and done this evil in Thy sight" (Ps. 51:4).

The Bible defines sin variously as "transgression of the Law" (1 John 3:4), as falling short of the mark (Rom. 3:23), and as failure to do the good we know we should do (James 4:17). Sin has both an active, overt aspect (transgression of the Law) and a passive aspect (failure to do good). There are sins of commission and sins of omission. The Book of Common Prayer adequately summarizes, in its General Confession, "We have done those things we ought not to have done and we have left undone those things we ought to have done."

The first sin was the prototype of all other sins. The seriousness of the first sin lies in the fact that Adam and Eve broke a commandment of God that showed His authority, goodness, wisdom, justice, faithfulness, and grace. In their transgression, they rejected His authority, doubted His goodness, disputed His wisdom, repudiated His justice, contradicted His truthfulness, and spurned His grace. Then and now, sin is the opposite of God's perfection.[34]

The seriousness of sin is based on man's alienation from and broken fellowship with God. It brought disastrous consequences to Adam, and to humanity and society in general. The root problem in the world today is not ignorance or poverty, as great as these are. The root problem is sin. Man is alienated from God, and hence is self-centered. The tensions between racial groups, economic classes, and nations are nothing more than the self-centeredness of the individual blown up on a wide canvas to include all men.

The Good News

If no power is strong enough to change human nature, there is no hope for man. But the good news of the Gospel is that there IS such power — in Christ. "Where sin abounded, grace did much more abound" (Rom. 5:20).

Unless we understand what the Bible teaches about the nature of man in creation and the devastating effects of the Fall, we cannot understand the grandeur of the grace of God. Many problems in understanding God's grace stem from an inflated view of man and his character and a shrunken view of God and His holiness.

These issues are matters of life and death. Man does not live and die like an animal. Death does not end man's existence. The soul and spirit survive the body. Jesus Himself spoke clearly of this continued existence for both the saved and the lost: "I am the Resurrection and the Life; he that believeth in Me, though he were dead, yet shall he live; and whosoever liveth and believeth in Me shall never die" (John 11:25, 26). In the story of the rich man and Lazarus (Luke 16:19-31), Christ clearly taught the continued conscious existence of the unjust. The whole teaching of the New Testament about future judgment rests on the assumption that the soul survives after death. "It is appointed unto men once to die, but after this the judgment" (Heb. 9:27; cf. Rom. 2:5-11; 2 Cor. 5:10).

The Resurrection applies not only to those who will be raised to be with Christ forever (1 Thess. 4:16), but also to the wicked, who will be raised for judgment. Jesus said clearly, "The hour is coming in the which *all* that are in the graves shall hear His voice and shall come forth; they that have done *good* unto the resurrection of life, and they that have done *evil* unto the resurrection of damnation" (John 5:28, 29).

The sobering truth that we exist forever makes it imperative that we give thought to our nature, condition, and destiny while we are still able to do what is needful.

In answer to the question "Who am I?" the Bible clearly answers that each of us is a personality created purposefully by God in His own image. It teaches that we have eternal significance and that our souls are worth more than the whole world (Mark 8:36). God Himself says that He has a plan and a purpose for each life, that we are morally responsible to respond to Him, and that we *can* respond in faith. We have an eternal destiny — either in His presence forever, or in everlasting separation from Him.

The Bible is the most realistic book ever written. It not only describes God as He really is, but us as we really are. It gives us a clear vision of our own nature and destiny, and that of the human race.

For Further Reading

Laidlaw, J. *The Bible Doctrine of Man.* Edinburgh: T. & T. Clark, 1905.

Leitch, Addison H. *The Creation of Matter, Life, and Man,* fifth in the "Fundamentals of the Faith" series. Washington: *Christianity Today*, Sept. 16, 1966.

Machen, J. G. *The Christian View of Man.* London: Banner of Truth, 1965.

Orr, James. *God's Image in Man.* Grand Rapids: Eerdmans, 1948.

Chapter 6

The Holy Spirit

Of the three persons in the Godhead — Father,
Son and Holy Spirit — the Holy Spirit seems to be
least known and understood today. Yet He is most
vitally and intimately involved in our initial conversion and birth into the family of God, as well
as in the ongoing development of our Christian
lives. Knowledge of and intimate relationship
with the Holy Spirit bring us power, joy, and hope.
When we neglect Him, through ignorance or indifference, we insure spiritual poverty.

It is of great importance that we be clear in
our minds that God the Holy Spirit is as much a
person as God the Father and God the Son. Many
Christians are inclined to speak of Him as an impersonal "it." They give the impression that the
Holy Spirit is no more than an influence. Perhaps
this is partially due to the fact that we use the
term "spirit," in casual conversation, in this sense.
We speak of the "spirit" of the times or say that

"a spirit of expectancy swept the crowd as they awaited the arrival of the President."

Misunderstanding may partially stem also from the fact that the work of the Holy Spirit is not as visibly prominent as that of the Father and of the Son. His work is never to call attention to Himself. Jesus, in speaking of the gift of the Spirit, said, "He shall not speak of Himself, but whatsoever He shall hear, that shall He speak. And He will show you things to come. He shall glorify Me: for He shall receive of Mine, and shall show it unto you" (John 16:13, 14).

Some of the names and symbols by which the Holy Spirit is called may seem to suggest that He is not a personal being. Both the Hebrew and Greek words translated "spirit" mean, basically, "breath" or "wind." The Greek word is in the neuter gender, which is why the King James version — adding to the confusion — translates "the Spirit *itself*" (Rom. 8:16, 26). Later versions read "Himself."

Impersonal Symbols

Then, too, the symbols used in Scripture to describe the influence of the Spirit include oil, fire, and water — all of which are impersonal. To a superficial student, these symbols could imply that the Spirit is merely an influence. Yet the Father and the Son are described in similar figurative ways — as light, bread of life, living water, etc.

When we speak of the personality of the Holy Spirit, however, we must remind ourselves of the significance of this term as applied to God. As we have observed, God was not made in the image of man, but man in the image of God. "Personality" is not a perfect term for use with God, but it is descriptive of the Spirit's nature. It is comforting to know that the Holy Spirit has a mind, feelings, and a will, as God the Father does. He is a *person* in this sense.

It is impossible to explain many biblical references to the Holy Spirit apart from the fact that He is equal, in His personal nature, to the Father and the Son.

Jesus gave some of the clearest scriptural teaching about the Holy Spirit. He called the Spirit the Comforter, or Counselor, "whom the Father will send in My name; He shall teach you all things and bring all things to your remembrance, whatsoever I have said unto you" (John 14:26). These titles clearly imply personality. The terms "Comforter," or "Counselor," convey the idea of a person, such as a lawyer, on whom one calls for help. Obviously, counseling and comforting would not be possible if the Spirit were merely an impersonal influence.

In John 16:7, as in the previous reference, the emphasis is on Christ's going away and the Holy Spirit's being sent by the Father to replace our Lord Himself. This change, Jesus said, would be beneficial for His disciples. An impersonal force could hardly improve on the personal presence of Jesus Christ.

Repeatedly (John 16:7-15), Jesus used the masculine personal pronoun "He" when referring to the Spirit. As we have pointed out, the Greek word translated "spirit" is the same as that for "breath," and is neuter in gender. Jesus used the masculine pronoun deliberately, intending it to indicate personality and intimacy.

Though the Holy Spirit is not mentioned with the Father and the Son in New Testament greetings and salutations (e.g., 1 Cor. 1:3; Gal. 1:3, etc.), He is mentioned in the baptismal formula. The Lord told the disciples, "Go ye therefore and teach all nations, baptizing them in the name of the Father and of the Son and of the Holy Spirit" (Matt. 28:19). The Spirit is also included in the Pauline benediction, "The grace of the Lord Jesus Christ, and the love of God, and the communion of the Holy Spirit be with you all" (2 Cor. 13:14). Association of the Holy Spirit with the other two Persons of the Trinity also appears in 1 Peter 1:1, 2 and in Jude 20, 21.

We can *treat* the Spirit as a *person.* Ananias was struck dead for lying to the Holy Spirit (Acts 5:3). The Spirit may be *grieved* (Eph. 4:30) and *sinned against* by unforgivable blasphemy (Mark 3:29). None of these things would be true of an impersonal force.

The Holy Spirit *does* things which only a person could do. He *speaks*: "The Spirit said unto Philip, 'Go near'" (Acts 8:29). He *strives*: "My Spirit shall not strive with man forever" (Gen. 6:3). "The Spirit also helpeth our infirmity . . . [and] *maketh intercession* for us" (Rom. 8:26). He *reveals, searches,* and *knows*: "But God hath revealed them unto us by His Spirit; for the Spirit searcheth all things . . . the things of God knoweth no man but the Spirit of God" (1 Cor. 2:10, 11). He distributes spiritual gifts "to every man severally as He will" (1 Cor. 12:11). None of these verbs could rightly be used of a mere influence.

Identified with Believers

The Holy Spirit is identified with the thinking of believers. At the Council of Jerusalem the disciples declared, "It seemed good to us *and* to the Holy Spirit" (cf. Acts 15:28).

The Holy Spirit is not only a person — He is Deity. He is specifically called "God" in the Ananias incident (Acts 5:4). Paul says, "For the Lord is that Spirit" (2 Cor. 3:17; cf. v. 18), and again, "Ye are the temple of God . . . the Spirit of God dwelleth in you" (1 Cor. 3:16).

Our Lord says that blasphemy against the Holy Spirit is worse than blasphemy against the Son of Man. This can only mean that blasphemy against the Spirit maligns and discredits God.

The Holy Spirit possesses attributes which belong only to Deity. He is *eternal*: "Christ, who through the eternal Spirit offered Himself" (Heb. 9:14). He is *omnipresent*: "Whither shall I go from Thy Spirit? or whither shall I flee from Thy presence?" (Ps. 139:7-10). He is the "Spirit of *life*" (Rom. 8:2) and the "Spirit of truth" (John 16:13).

The Spirit does God's work. He was involved in *creation*: "the Spirit of God moved upon the . . . waters" (Gen. 1:2). He is involved in *regenera-*

tion, the new birth: "So is everyone that is born of the Spirit" (John 3:8). Jesus cast out demons by the Spirit: "I cast out [demons] by the Spirit of God" (Matt. 12:28). The Holy Spirit participates in *resurrection*: "But if the Spirit of Him that raised up Jesus from the dead dwell in you, He . . . shall also quicken your mortal bodies by His Spirit that dwelleth in you" (Rom. 8:11).

The New Testament quotes many Old Testament passages in which the speaker is Jehovah, the Lord. In the New Testament, such messages are often attributed to the Holy Spirit. For instance, Isaiah heard the voice of the Lord saying, "Hear ye indeed but understand not" (Isa. 6:8, 9). But Paul said, "Well spoke *the Holy Spirit* by Isaiah the prophet unto our fathers, saying . . . 'Hearing ye shall hear and shall not understand'" (Acts 28: 25-26).

Just as the truth of the Trinity is hinted at in the Old Testament but awaits its fullest expression in the New, so with truth about the Holy Spirit. His personality and deity are evident in the Old Testament, but the full expression of His activity is given only in the New Testament. There is no conflict here with the Old Testament, but the New Testament picture is much more complete.

Old Testament teaching

Five differing aspects of the work of the Spirit are discernible in the Old Testament:[35]

1. The work of the Spirit in the creation of the universe (Gen. 1:2) and of man: "The Spirit of

God hath made me, and the breath of the Almighty hath given me life" (Job 33:4).

2. The work of the Spirit in equipping for service. He conferred power on judges and warriors. For instance, "The Spirit of the Lord came mightily upon [Samson]" (Jud. 14:6). The Israelites cried out to God and He gave them Othniel, "and the Spirit of the Lord came upon him, and he judged Israel and went out to war" (Jud. 3:10). When the Spirit came upon people for a particular purpose in this manner, He did not necessarily transform their moral character.

Wisdom and skill for particular jobs, including those of a nonspiritual nature, were imparted to various individuals by the Spirit. Bezaleel was filled with the Spirit to work in gold, silver, and brass for the Tabernacle (Ex. 31:3-5).

3. The work of the Spirit in inspiring the prophets. Usually they began their message with, "Thus saith the Lord." At times, however, they also attributed their message to the Holy Spirit: "And the Spirit entered into me when He spake unto me, and set me upon my feet" (Ezek. 2:2). And Moses exclaimed, "Enviest thou for *my* sake? Would God that all the Lord's people were prophets and that the Lord would put His Spirit upon them!" (Num. 11:29)

Moral Living

4. The work of the Holy Spirit in producing moral living. David, in agony of repentance for his dual sin of adultery and murder, pleaded for

God to create a clean heart in him, and begged, "Take not Thy Holy Spirit from me" (Ps. 51:11). The Spirit, David knew, is good, and He leads men to do God's will (Ps. 143:10). Because of the presence of God's Spirit, which David sensed is inescapable, he pleaded for a searching of his heart and for clear leading in the eternal way (Ps. 139:7, 23, 24).

5. The work of the Spirit in foretelling the coming of the Messiah. The references which anticipate Christ are of two kinds. First are those which prophesy a direct indwelling of the Spirit in one messianic figure: "The Spirit of the Lord God is upon Me, because the Lord hath anointed Me to preach good tidings" (Isa. 61:1). Jesus read this passage in the synagogue at Nazareth and uttered the electrifying words, "This day is this Scripture fulfilled in your ears" (Luke 4:21; cf. Luke 4:18; Isa. 9:2-9; 42:1-4).

The second way the Holy Spirit anticipated Christ was in the more general way of speaking about the new covenant people of God. "A new heart also will I give you, and a new Spirit will I put within you" (Ezek. 36:26; cf. v. 27). Both this prophecy and the comprehensive promise to Joel speak of the Spirit being given to all classes: "And . . . I will pour out My Spirit upon all flesh" (Joel 2:28; cf. v. 29).

Equips for a Task

The Old Testament's earlier teaching on the Holy Spirit emphasized the coming of the Spirit to equip a person to perform a certain task. The Scripture suggests that out of this bestowal of the Spirit, men grew more conscious of their inner need for God's help if they were to be morally pure enough to serve the Lord. Later in the Old Testament period, some scholars detect an awareness, on the part of believers, that the human government of Israel would never succeed in achieving the purposes of Jehovah, and a growing realization that, in time, the Spirit would be given to all God's people.[36]

Glimpses of the person and work of the Holy Spirit in the Old Testament are numerous and clear. However, the Old Testament period could not be called "the age of the Spirit" as our age, since the coming of the Holy Spirit in fulness on the Day of Pentecost, is called. Before Pentecost the Spirit came on particular people for particular tasks. While men could have an intimate relationship with Him, as shown by David's experience, the fellowship was not as personal or as permanent as is possible since Pentecost. The Spirit came upon individuals temporarily and then, when the occasion for His coming was over, withdrew. Samson's tragic downfall resulted from the Spirit's withdrawal. Samson had become so insensitive that he was not even aware that the Spirit had left him (Jud. 16:20). Nor was the experience of the Spirit in that era as widespread or universal as it is now, when He indwells everyone who is in the Church of Jesus Christ by the new birth. It is emphatically true that "if any man have not the Spirit of Christ, he is none of His" (Rom. 8:9).

Our Lord's words to the disciples in this connection are instructive: "[The Spirit] dwelleth *with* you and shall be *in* you" (John 14:17). Just as there was a dispute in the Church, during the Arian controversy, over the Trinity and whether or not the Son of God had existed eternally or was the first of God's creatures, so there was also conflict concerning the Holy Spirit. In the Nicene Creed He is called, "The Lord, the Life-Giver, that proceeds from the Father, that with the Father and Son is together worshipped and together glorified." This formula was finally adopted by the Council of Chalcedon in A.D. 451.

"Procession" and "Generation"

The phrase "proceeds from the Father" is taken from the Gospel of John: "But when the Comforter is come, whom I will send unto you from the Father, even the Spirit of truth, which proceedeth from the Father, He shall testify of Me" (15:26). This and other statements (e.g., John 16: 7; 14:16; 20:22; etc.) imply a type of subordination of the Spirit to the Father and Son. This is only a subordination of relationship, not of Deity.

Neither "generation" nor "procession" indicate a lack of equality within the Godhead, nor do they imply a creation or beginning of existence. Rather, they imply an eternal relation to the Father. They are "not a relation in any way analogous to physical derivation, but a life-movement of the divine nature, in virtue of which Father, Son, and Holy Spirit, while equal in essence and dignity, stand to each other in order of personality, office, and operation, and in virtue of which the Father works through the Son, and the Father and Son through the Spirit."[37]

In the year A.D. 589 the words, "and from the Son" were added to the Nicene Creed. This addition created tremendous controversy. The Western Church insisted on the addition to insure the preservation of the scriptural teaching that the Holy Spirit is the Spirit of Christ as well as of the Father. The Eastern Church refuses this insertion, feeling that it weakens the doctrine of subordination and makes our Lord a separate source of Deity. But "the union of the Father and the Son in 'sending' the Spirit really works against any idea of differentiation which would mar the inner harmony of the divine Triad. . . . Scripture seems clearly to state that while the Spirit proceeds from the Father, He was also 'given' by the Son to His Church, and that He is as much the Spirit of Christ as the Spirit of God."[38]

Some of the references that clarify and reinforce the concepts of the Spirit's Deity and personality are: "The Spirit of God dwelleth in you" (1 Cor. 3:16); "the Spirit of Christ" (Rom. 8:9); and "God hath sent forth the Spirit of His Son into your hearts" (Gal. 4:6).

His Other Titles

Other descriptive titles of the Holy Spirit include "the Spirit of grace" (Heb. 10:29); "the Spirit of Truth" (cf. 1 John 5:6); "the Spirit of wisdom and understanding, the Spirit of counsel and might, the Spirit of knowledge and of the fear of the Lord" (Isa. 11:2). He is the "Spirit of promise," that is, the One who came in fulfillment of Christ's promise (Eph. 1:13). He is also "the Spirit of glory" (1 Peter 4:14).

The Holy Spirit, then, is completely personal and completely God. He is coequal and coeternal with the Father and the Son.

We have already seen glimpses of the Spirit's work. We shall now look at it more closely. Though the Holy Spirit is self-effacing, His is the direct work of God and vitally affects each of us as individuals. He is active at various levels. In general, the Holy Spirit functions as the Executor of the purposes and plans of the Godhead. He is the One who carries out God's purposes — creation, conviction, regeneration, enlightenment, sanctification, and glorification.

In relationship to the world, the Spirit took part in the creation of the universe, as already mentioned in our review of His Old Testament activities. He is also referred to as the Preserver of nature: "Thou sendest forth Thy Spirit, [the fish] are created: and Thou renewest the face of the earth" (Ps. 104:29, 30; cf. Isa. 40:7).

Jesus outlined the work of the Spirit so far as humanity as a whole is concerned. He convicts the world of sin, of righteousness, and of judgment (John 16:8-11). As we saw in Chapter 1, the Holy Spirit is the Author of the Scriptures, the One who inspired them (2 Peter 1:20, 21). He is also the One who interprets them and applies them to our hearts at a particular time. He is the Spirit of wisdom and revelation (Eph. 1:17), and He interprets the mind of God (1 Cor. 2:9-14). It has been rightly observed that this "illuminating" work of the Holy Spirit never becomes so mystical and subjective that grammatical and historical consistency are abandoned. By misunderstanding the role of the Holy Spirit in interpreting the Word, some have made the Bible almost a magical book, equating their subjective feelings with the authority of the Spirit.

The Spirit and Christ

The Holy Spirit had a particularly intimate relationship with the Lord Jesus Christ, who in His humanity was completely dependent on the Spirit. He was *conceived* by the Holy Spirit and *born* of Him (Luke 1:35). Jesus was *led* by the Spirit (Matt. 4:1). He was *anointed* for His ministry by the Spirit in a special way at His baptism (Matt. 3:13-17). He *offered* Himself as a sacrifice through the Spirit (Heb. 9:14), and He was *raised* from the dead by the power of the Spirit (Rom. 1:4). He gave *commandments* to the apostles, and through them to the Church, by the Spirit (Acts 1:2).

In the Church, the Holy Spirit administers spiritual gifts for the good of the whole body: "But the manifestation of the Spirit is given to every man to profit withal" (1 Cor. 12:7; cf. entire chapter). He is the dynamic power which was promised the Church before Pentecost: "Ye shall receive power, after that the Holy Spirit has come upon you" (Acts 1:8). Because of the phenomenal exploits of the Early Church, which turned the Roman world upside down, The Acts has been called "The Acts of the Holy Spirit."

Through the work of the Holy Spirit in the individual Christian, a believer comes into the most intimate personal contact with God.

The Holy Spirit is the One who brings conviction of sin to an individual (John 16:8). Whenever a person comes to a sense of his own sinfulness, whether by the preached, written, or personally spoken word, the Spirit of God has been at work.

The Spirit's Sealing

As soon as a person puts his trust in Christ He is "sealed" by the Holy Spirit (Eph. 1:13). A seal is a symbol of a finished transaction, of ownership, and of security. Because we are sealed by the Spirit, we can have certainty and assurance of salvation. "The Spirit Himself beareth witness with our spirit that we are the children of God" (cf. Rom. 8:16).

The Spirit indwells each individual Christian, whose body is the Spirit's temple. Along with the Incarnation and Resurrection, here is another indication from Scripture that the human body is not inherently evil or sinful. It also reminds us that we are to take our bodies seriously. They are never to be in any way mutilated, abused, or neglected. There is no place in the Scripture for the kind of asceticism which punishes the body in the interests of "spirituality." Extreme forms of such self-affliction occurred at different periods of Church History, particularly in medieval times, and more sophisticated forms are with us even today.

We are sealed and indwelt by the Holy Spirit at the time we are baptized by the Spirit, "for by one Spirit we are all baptized into one body, whether we be Jews or Gentiles, whether we be bond or free, and have been all made to drink of one Spirit" (1 Cor. 12:13). This baptism, with its attendant sealing and indwelling by the Spirit, takes place at the time of conversion. This participation in the Spirit is shared by *all* believers, despite their varying degrees of maturity, strength, and devotion.

Some Christians, however, apply the term "baptism" to one's first experience of being *filled* with the Spirit, which experience is part of God's purpose for us (Eph. 5:18).

No one is a Christian who does not have the Holy Spirit (Rom. 8:7), for He indwells and seals *every* believer. Unfortunately, however, many Christians never know the joy and power of the Holy Spirit's fullness.

Filled with the Spirit

This being filled with the Spirit is not a once-for-all experience, but one that may be repeated. On the Day of Pentecost the disciples were filled with the Spirit (Acts 2:4). A few days later, in

113

a dramatic prayer meeting, they had such an experience again (4:31).

The filling of the Spirit implies being given power and boldness for God's service, and strength to meet particular crises. It is possible, and it sometimes happens, that the baptism of the Spirit and the infilling of the Spirit take place at the same time. They need not be separated in experience. But the filling of the Spirit is an experience to be repeated as necessary in the life of each believer. We are, literally, to "keep on being filled" (cf. Eph. 5:8, lit.).

The Holy Spirit is not a substance, but a Person. The fullness of the Spirit is not a matter of our receiving more of Him. Rather, it is a matter of relationship. To be filled with the Spirit means we allow Him to occupy, guide, and control every area of our lives. His power can then work through us, making us effectively fruitful for God and flooding our hearts with His joy. This filling applies not only to our outward acts but to our inner thoughts and motives. When we are filled with the Spirit, all we are and have is subject to His control.

The test as to whether or not you are filled with the Spirit is not, "Have you received an external sign or been given a particular gift of the Spirit?" Rather, Have you given yourself wholly and without reservation to God? (Rom. 12:1) Are you genuinely willing that He should control, absolutely and entirely, your life? Many believers come to a point of utter frustration in their service for the Lord simply because they fail to realize the need to be filled with the Spirit if they are to act in God's power. Just as we cannot *save* ourselves apart from the work of the Holy Spirit, neither can we *live* the life of victory or serve the Lord effectively without the Spirit. When we learn to trust Him fully, allowing Him to work through us, we are freed from the frustration of trying to accomplish spiritual and eternal results solely through our human ability — or, more properly, inability.

It is the Holy Spirit who delivers us from the power of sin. "For the law of the Spirit of life in Christ Jesus has made me free from the law of sin and death" (Rom. 8:2). The Holy Spirit changes the *pattern* of our life so that we *can* overcome sin. He does not make us sinless (1 John 1:8), but in Him we are able to start fulfilling the righteousness of the Law (Rom. 8:4). Such holy living is a work of the Spirit and a *result* of salvation; it is not in any way the *basis* for our being saved.

The Spirit's Fruit

When the Holy Spirit produces His fruit in us, we find that "love, joy, peace, patience, gentleness, goodness, faithfulness, meekness, and self-control" (cf. Gal. 5:22, 23) come naturally to us instead of our having to labor strenuously to cultivate these traits.

The Holy Spirit is also a guide to the individual Christian. We are instructed to "walk in the Spirit" (Gal. 5:16). His leadership is one of the signs that an individual is really a child of God: "For as

115

many as are led by the Spirit of God, they are the sons of God" (Rom. 8:14). The Holy Spirit clearly led and guided the early Christians, as we read in The Acts, and He does the same today if a Christian is open and sensitive to His control.

The Holy Spirit prays for us (Rom. 8:26). What a wonderful thing to realize, especially when *we* don't know how to pray, that the Spirit of God makes intercession for us!

The opposite of this intimate, loving, dynamic relationship with the Holy Spirit is experienced when we offend Him. We are not to "grieve" the Spirit (Eph. 4:30). To grieve is to make sad. In the verses immediately following this command, some of the things that grieve the Spirit are enumerated. They have to do with attitudes, thoughts, words, and actions. Other things also grieve God's Spirit — idolatry, hatred, strife, heresy, envy, etc. (Gal. 5:18-21). To withhold anything from Him is to grieve Him. It is a solemn thing to realize that even as *we* can be grieved, we can also, in a much more profound way, grieve God's Holy Spirit.

We are commanded, "Quench not the Spirit" (1 Thes. 5:19). Because the figure of quenching suggests the idea of fire, some believe that this sin is more related to outward service than to motives and attitudes. In the scriptural context it suggests both. The verse follows a call to rejoice, pray, and give thanks. It precedes a warning not to despise whatever claims to be of God, but to test it. We may not only quench the Spirit in ourselves, but, by sinful living, confused beliefs, and unconcern may quench His work in and for others as well. On the other hand, the Spirit may well use others to correct, enlighten, and encourage *us*. To fail to receive God's Word through another person simply because he, like us, is imperfect, is to quench God's own Holy Spirit.

Through the Holy Spirit we *come* to know Christ, and by the Holy Spirit's power we *live* and *grow* in Christ, in the service of the King and in the fellowship of His Church.

For Further Reading

Morgan, G. Campbell. *The Spirit of God.* London: H. E. Walter, 1953.

Morris, Leon. *Spirit of the Living God.* Chicago: Inter-Varsity Press, 1960.

Ryle, J. C. *Holiness.* Edinburgh: James Clarke, 1952.

Thomas, W. H. Griffith. *The Holy Spirit of God.* Grand Rapids: Eerdmans, 1955.

Chapter 7

The Church

A great many ecclesiastical leaders today are admittedly uncertain as to just what the Church is. One modern theologian has written a book whose title sums up what is in the minds of many people: *The Misunderstanding of the Church.* Small wonder, then, that confusion about the Church is common in the minds of "ordinary" Christians, especially in view of the increasing extent to which "the Church" is in the news. The ecumenical movement is increasingly influential, and denominational mergers are occurring with more frequency than had been thought possible.

Among (and sometimes even *within*) the various groups of "Christians," there is considerable difference of opinion about matters of form, church government, mode of baptism, essential doctrines, etc. Some competing groups profess to be "the *one* 'true' Church." It is especially important, in view of all the conflicting voices heard today, that every

Christian know what the Bible teaches about the Church.

In the New Testament, the Greek word *ekklēsia,* translated "church," means a "called out" group, or "assembly" — not necessarily a religious one. The Ephesus town clerk, trying to quell a near-riot, said, "If ye enquire anything concerning other matters, it shall be determined in a lawful assembly [*ekklēsia*]" (Acts 19:39).

Applied to Christians, "the Church" means those who have been called out to Jesus Christ. In the New Testament it "mostly means a local congregation of Christians, and never a building. . . . Although we often speak of these congregations collectively as the New Testament Church, or the Early Church, no New Testament writer uses *ekklēsia* in this collective way. Its commonest use was for the public assembly of citizens duly summoned, which was a feature of all the cities outside Judea where the Gospel was planted."[39] The term also applied to the Universal Church, the body of Christ: "[God] hath put all things under [Christ's] feet, and gave Him to be head over all things to the *Church,* which is His body" (Eph. 1:22, 23).

The New Testament Church, then, is defined in two ways. First, it is "the whole company of regenerate persons . . . in heaven and on earth" (Matt. 16:18; Eph. 5:24, 25; Heb. 12:23).[40] This is the universal invisible Church. It is universal in that it includes all true believers in every place, and those who have gone on as well as those still alive. It is invisible in that it is not apparent in its entirety at any given time or place.

Second, there is also the individual local group, or church, through which the Universal Church is evident. "The individual church may be defined as that smaller company of regenerate persons who, in any given community, unite themselves voluntarily together in accordance with Christ's laws, for the purpose of securing the complete establishment of His kingdom in themselves and in the world."[41]

People in View

In both definitions, *people* are in view — not buildings. Today we use the word "church" in several additional ways. In answer to the question, "Where is your church?" we are more likely to answer, "At 18th and Green Streets" than "At County Hospital, Joe's Texaco Station, Motorola, and Circle Campus." A church is where its members are at any given time. Part of our problem, in reaching the world today, results from our "building" mentality. When we think of the activities of the church we tend to think only of what goes on within the four walls of the church building, rather than what takes place *in the world* through what believers say, do, and *are*.

God has always had His people. From the time of the Fall, when God gave Adam and Eve His promise of the Redeemer (Gen. 3:15), all who have believed His promises have been His people. God called Abraham and promised him, "I will

bless them that bless thee, and curse him that
curseth thee: and in thee shall all families of the
earth be blessed" (Gen. 12:3). He established an
eternal covenant with the nation of Israel as His
"chosen people." They were not chosen because of
inherent superiority over other racial or ethnic
groups. "The Lord did not set His love upon you,
nor choose you, because ye were more in number
than any people, for ye were the fewest of all people, but because the Lord loved you, and because
He would keep the oath which He had sworn unto
your fathers" (Deut. 7:7, 8).

Merely being born into the nation of Israel did
not make a person one of God's people spiritually:
"For he is not a Jew, which is one outwardly;
neither is that circumcision which is outward in the
flesh; but he is a Jew which is one in the Spirit,
and not in the letter" (Rom. 2:28, 29). Many who
were not Jews physically became Jews spiritually
by recognizing Jehovah as the true and living God
and turning from idols to Him. Perhaps the most
dramatic example of conversion to Judaism was in
the days of Esther, after the Jews' deliverance
from Haman. "In every province and in every city,
whithersoever the King's commandment and his
decree came, the Jews had joy and gladness, a
feast and a good day. And many of the people of
the land became Jews" (Es. 8:17). The occasion is
still celebrated today in the Feast of Purim.

Members of the Church are to have an intimate
relationship with each other as well as to Christ.
Therefore what hurts one member will hurt all,

and when one member is honored, all the others will rejoice with him (cf. 1 Cor. 12:26).

The Church was first mentioned by Jesus: "Upon this rock I will build My Church; and the gates of hell shall not prevail against it" (Matt. 16:18). On another occasion He described the simplest form of a church, saying, "Where two or three are gathered in My name, there am I in the midst of them" (Matt. 18:20).

Began at Pentecost

The Christian Church, as such, came into being with the coming of the Holy Spirit on the Day of Pentecost. After Peter's sermon on that occasion, "they that received his word were baptized; and there were added unto them in that day about three thousand souls. And they continued steadfastly in the apostles' teaching and fellowship, in the breaking of bread and the prayers. . . . And the Lord added to them day by day those that were being saved" (Acts 2:41, 42, 47, asv, marg.). The Church was born in Jerusalem. It at first consisted mainly of Jews who recognized Jesus as the Messiah. Many of them were Hellenists — that is, Greek-speaking Jews — who had been scattered all over the empire. Many came to Jerusalem regularly as pilgrims.

The Church was at first considered a sect within Judaism. One of Paul's accusers referred to him "as a mover of sedition among all the Jews throughout the world, and a ringleader of the sect of the Nazarenes" (Acts 24:5). The Roman government gave Christians the same exemption from military service it gave the Jews. The first Jewish Christians in Jerusalem continued to recognize their obligations to the Mosaic Law and still participated in the worship services of the Temple or synagogue.

Increasingly, however, Jewish proselytes (Gentiles who had embraced Judaism) believed the Gospel and came into the Church. Philip preached the good news in Samaria and later baptized an Ethiopian to whom he had witnessed (Acts 8). Only after a vision from the Lord did the universal scope of the Gospel finally get through to reluctant Peter (Acts 10:9-16). He later explained to Cornelius, a Gentile, that it had been "unlawful for a Jew to keep company or come unto one of another nation; but God hath showed me that I should not call any man common or unclean" (v. 28).

On hearing Cornelius' declaration of faith, Peter uttered the historic words, "Of a truth I perceive that God is no respecter of persons; but in every nation He that feareth Him and worketh righteousness is accepted with Him" (v. 34, 35). As if to vouch for the truth of what Peter was saying, the Holy Spirit came on his listeners, most of whom were Gentiles, as he spoke. The Jews with Peter were amazed that Gentiles also received the Holy Spirit, but Peter baptized them.

Other Christian Jews preached the Gospel in Antioch, where a mixed church of Jews and Gentiles came into existence (Acts 13:1). It was here that believers were first called Christians (Acts 11: 26), or "Christ's men."

123

What relationship Gentile converts should have to the Law and circumcision was the first great question the Early Church had to decide. A council held in Jerusalem made the momentous declaration, "For it seemed good to the Holy Spirit and to us to lay upon you no greater burden than these necessary things; that ye abstain from meats offered to idols, and from blood, and from things strangled, and from fornication, from which if ye keep yourselves ye shall do well" (Acts 15:28, 29).

New Testament Figures

The figures used in the New Testament to describe the Church are instructive. One is the "body of Christ." Christ is the head of the body. Every member functions under His leadership and in dependence on each other member. "For as the body is one, and hath many members, and all the members of that one body, being many, are one body, so also is Christ" (1 Cor. 12:12; cf. Eph. 4:4; Col. 3:15).

Christ leads the Church, and it is to be subject to Him (Eph. 5:23, 24). He is the source of its unity — "for ye are all one in Christ Jesus" (Gal. 3:28). Some Christians make few practical applications of this unity.

The Church is also compared to a building: "Ye [believers] also, as living stones, are built up a spiritual house, an holy priesthood" (1 Peter 2:5). This household of God is "built upon the foundation of the apostles and prophets, Jesus Christ Himself being the chief Cornerstone" (Eph. 2:20). This building, or temple, is the dwelling place of the Holy Spirit; it is comprised of all individuals indwelt by the Holy Spirit (1 Cor. 6:19 ff.). God Himself dwells within the Church, so whoever attacks the Church attacks God. In criticizing the Church, we must be careful we are not criticizing God.

The Church is called the Bride of Christ. Marriage illustrates Christ's relationship to the Church (Eph. 5:25-27, 31, 32; cf. 2 Cor. 11:2; Rev. 19:7; 22:17). This figure powerfully displays Christ's intense love for His Church and His total commitment to her.

The Church in the New Testament apparently was relatively simple. There were no denominations, though Paul rebuked party spirit among the Christians in Corinth (1 Cor. 3:3-8). How, then, have we come to the complex situation in which we find the Church today?

There are, of course, numerous historical reasons, such as persecutions, heresy, and formation of national churches. But part of the reason for the development of differing groups of believers is the fact that the New Testament gives only limited instruction about church organization and practice. Sincere Christians, all claiming scriptural authority, have always differed in the interpretation of certain passages and teachings of the New Testament. It is important, therefore, to trace the discernible lines of the New Testament Church pattern and to understand some of the major interpretations of them.

Membership Requirements

Requirements for Church membership are implicit in The Acts. The first was belief in the Lord Jesus Christ (Acts 2:38). Faith in Christ, which normally includes repentance for sin, is the spiritual prerequisite to new life and membership in the body of Christ. When people asked Jesus the question, "What shall we do, that we might work the works of God?" He answered, "This is the work of God, that ye believe on Him whom He hath sent" (John 6:28, 29).

Baptism was to follow faith, as an open confession of trust in Christ, though some earnest Christians believe that the "one baptism" (Eph. 4:5) is the baptism of the Holy Spirit, and that water baptism is not God's purpose for Christians today.

Adherence to revealed truth, among early Christians, was the standard. "And they continued stedfastly in the apostles' doctrine and fellowship, and in breaking of bread and in prayers" (Acts 2:42). Paul warns of false teachers arising within the Church (Phil. 3:2), and Peter echoes the same solemn theme. Throughout the New Testament there is emphasis on doctrinal purity and holiness of life. Doctrinal and moral impurity are to be purged from the Church (1 Cor. 5:7).

God's "called out" people were designated "saints" (Eph. 1:1; 1 Cor. 1:2; Phil. 1:1). They met together for worship and mutual upbuilding of spiritual life (1 Cor. 14:3, 5, 19; Col. 3:16). The Church was an evangelizing fellowship whose purpose was the communication and preservation of the Gospel message throughout the whole world (Matt. 28:19, 20; Acts 1:8). Paul's letters placed little stress on evangelism, possibly because early believers were naturally and effectively evangelistic. He wrote to the Thessalonians, "For from you sounded out the word of the Lord not only in Macedonia and Achaia, but also in every place your faith toward God is spread abroad, so that we need not to speak anything" (1 Thes. 1:8, sco).

Christians were to be servants, meeting the physical and spiritual needs of both believers and unbelievers. "As we have therefore opportunity, let us do good unto all men, especially unto them who are of the household of faith" (Gal. 6:10). Christ Himself was the example; He "went about doing good" (Acts 10:38).

As Leon Morris puts it, "During the history of the Church there have been many variations from the New Testament pattern. Indeed, there are so many gaps in our knowledge of what went on in New Testament times that we cannot be quite sure what constituted that pattern. Even those groups who claim to model their polity exactly on the New Testament cannot be certain they have succeeded. . . . No attempt seems to have been made to fasten any pattern on succeeding generations, for no authoritative directions were given as to the mode and perpetuation of the ministry. Ministerial forms have evolved in a variety of ways."[42]

That there was some organization at the local level in New Testament times seems clear. There were stated meetings (Acts 20:7); elected deacons (Acts 6:5, 6); membership discipline (1 Cor. 5:13); letters of commendation (Acts 18:27); and lists of widows for support (1 Tim. 5:9).

God gave spiritual gifts to the Church. "He gave some, apostles; and some, prophets; and some, evangelists; and some, pastors and teachers; for the perfecting of the saints for the work of the ministry, for the edifying of the body of Christ" (Eph. 4:11, 12). The purpose of these gifts is "the perfection of the saints for the work of the ministry." There is no clear distinction between clergy and laity, either in terms of church government or spiritual ministry.

Periods of Ministry

Hammond outlines the three periods in the New Testament ministry:[43]

1. *The first period.* (a) Our Lord's ministry with the 70 whom He commissioned; (b) the apostolic ministry of those who had specially delegated authority from the Lord to give authoritative leadership in the Church after Pentecost; and (c) the ministry of deacons, elders, and bishops. The three pastoral epistles (1, 2 Tim.; Titus) give the principles of and qualifications for the ministry.

2. *The transitional period.* During most of the lifetime of the apostles, and until the New Testament had been circulated to the various Christian communities, there were special gifts, such as prophecy, in the Church. The object of these was to enable the local community to receive the

New Testament revelation of Christ direct from the Spirit of God. When the apostles had completed their work, some of these "gifts" ceased. For instance, there was not an unending succession of apostles and prophets (cf. Eph. 2:20; 3:5; 4:11).

3. *The permanent ministry.* A bishop, or elder, was to teach spiritual truth and exercise rule and discipline in the local church (1 Tim. 5:17; Heb. 13:7). "Remember them which have the rule over you, who have spoken unto you the Word of God: whose faith follow, considering the end of their manner of life" (Heb. 13:17, sco; cf. 1 Tim. 5:17).

Deacons helped in administering the business of a church (Acts 6:1-6; 1 Tim. 3:8-12), though it is clear there are spiritual overtones to their activity.

In view of the many denominations and sects throughout Church History, it is surprising that all forms of Church government and views of the ministry fall generally into one of three groupings: the episcopal,* the presbyterial, or the congregational.[44]

Episcopalianism

In the episcopalian system, the church is governed by bishops, but there are also presbyters (or priests) and deacons. The only one in this

---

*These terms, as here used, refer to systems of church government rather than to denominations.

system who has power to ordain is the bishop. The bishops trace their office back many centuries. Some, in fact, claim to trace the line back to the apostles — hence the term so often used: "apostolic succession." Among other groups, the Roman Catholic, Orthodox, Anglican, Episcopal, Methodist, and some Lutheran churches have the episcopal form of government.

This system is admittedly not found in the New Testament. A full episcopalian system had not yet developed. Those who hold to this type of church government, however, feel that it was a natural development in the Second Century Church. They see, in the work of some New Testament figures, a transition between the itinerant ministry of the apostles and the more settled ministry of the later bishops. Timothy and Titus had a good deal of authority over a number of churches, yet lacked the wide apostolic authority of Paul. James of Jerusalem was, it is felt, an example of an apostle who had a localized ministry but was more like a later bishop than like Paul. The development of episcopacy is traced through the Early Church Fathers.

It is significant, many feel, that there is no trace of a struggle to establish the episcopalian system. If a divinely established presbyterial or congregational system had been overthrown, it is argued, a bitter conflict between the two factions would have been inevitable. By the Second Century, however, without any such conflict, the episcopal system predominated throughout the whole Church.

Presbyterianism

In presbyterianism, the Church is governed by elders. Presbyterians recognize that in the New Testament the term "elder" and "bishop" are used interchangeably and that they are clearly the most important element in the local ministry. In each local church, it would seem, a number of elders formed a kind of committee to handle church affairs. Elders in New Testament times acted with the apostles (Acts 15) — an indication of their importance. When the apostles passed from the scene, elders were the leading officers.

The local congregation seems also to have had a voice in the selection of men for the ministry. They chose the seven deacons (Acts 6:1-6) and apparently had a hand in setting aside Paul and Barnabas for missionary work (13:1-3). Presbyterians believe in the equality of elders, in the right of the people to take part (through their representatives) in the government of a church, and in the unity of the Church through a graduated series of church courts which express and exercise the common authority of the Church as a divine society.

John Dall distinguishes presbyterianism from the other two systems as follows: "As opposed to prelacy, the presbyterial type of government rests upon the equality of ministerial status and seeks to give ecclesiastical power to the members of the Church instead of to clerical individuals or councils; as opposed to congregationalism, it seeks to realize the unity of the Church by entrusting to a carefully devised system of graded church courts legislative, executive, and judicial — not merely advisory — powers."[45]

Presbyterians usually make a distinction between teaching and ruling elders (1 Tim. 5:17). The teaching elder is the principal order of ministry. He is ordained by the laying on of the hands of other elders. This is, in the presbyterial view, ordination to the universal Church and not to some small section of it.

Ruling elders are chosen by the congregation and admitted to their office by ordination. They may not preach, baptize, or administer communion, but they assist in the government of the church and in the exercise of discipline. They also have responsibility for the financial affairs of the church. Some presbyterians feel that the office of ruling elder is the same as that of teaching elder, but others regard ruling elders as laymen.

Presbyterians account for the development of a universal episcopal system by saying that "monarchial" bishops gained the supremacy over presbyters in the Church just after the apostolic age. They explain that church problems involving persecution and heresy could more easily be met by such a central authority. But this development, presbyterians maintain, was not in harmony with the essential nature of the ministry as revealed in the New Testament. They also believe that their system preserves the "episcopacy" through its "moderators" and general assembly, and that this preservation is not at the expense of ministerial equality.

Congregationalism

The third basic form of Church government is congregationalism. Every group whose emphasis is on the autonomy of the local congregation would be included here. Such groups include Baptists, the Open Brethren, Christians (Disciples), Evangelical Free Churches, and some Bible and other independent Churches. Followers of this polity hold that no man or group of men should exercise authority over a local congregation of Christ's Church. With some exceptions, these churches have two types of ministers — pastors and deacons. Pastors have oversight of the congregation. They are usually ordained or set apart in a service attended by representatives of other similar congregations, though neither their participation nor approval is necessary. Deacons (or, sometimes, elders) are generally assigned the responsibility of watching over the spiritual and material needs of the local congregation. Their office is usually regarded as purely local. Congregationalists, as most other Protestants, deny that ordination imparts special grace to a man.

Two basic ideas are behind the congregational view of the ministry. One is that Christ is the Head of His Church and, as such, is in living and vital contact with it. As our physical heads need no intermediary to control our bodies, so it is with the Head of the Church and *His* body. It is not two or three officials, but two or three *believers*, gathered together in His name, in whose midst Christ promises to be (Matt. 18:20).

The second basic idea, common to most other Protestants as well, is the priesthood of all believers (cf. 1 Peter 2:9). Strictly speaking, there are no laymen in the Church. All believers are priests (1 Peter 2:9) — that is, representatives of God to witness and minister to men in His name and power.

Further, the emphasis in the New Testament seems to be on the local church. There is no evidence of presbyterial or episcopal control of the Church as a whole. Bishops and elders appear to have exercised their control within a local congregation, but not beyond it. The episcopal system did not appear until the Second Century.

Almost all churches fit into one of the above three groupings so far as polity is concerned.

Church Ordinances

There are numerous differences of opinion about the number and nature of "ordinances" in the Church. Ordinances — some call them "sacraments" — are outward rites that signify or represent spiritual grace or blessing. The Roman Catholic Church has seven sacraments: baptism, the Lord's Supper, confirmation, penance, orders, matrimony, and extreme unction. Protestants maintain, however, that Scripture recognizes only two ordinances — baptism and the Lord's Supper.

Roman Catholics teach that objective merit or grace is conferred by the sacraments. In contrast to this mechanical, almost magical, view, most

Protestants emphasize faith and the working of God directly in the believer.

The meaning of baptism is perhaps most fully explained in Romans 6:1-4 (though some Christians insist that this chapter does not have baptism with water in view). Baptism has been called "an outward sign of an inward grace," a declaration and public identification with Christ in His death, burial, and resurrection. Protestants are divided on whether baptism should be administered only to those who are believers, who in it make a public profession of faith, or whether infants also should be baptized. Episcopalians, Presbyterians, Lutherans, Methodists, and others practice infant baptism. Baptists, Disciples, and a great number of independent churches, hold to believers' baptism only. The former group use various modes of baptizing; the latter use immersion.

Most Christians agree on their obligation to observe the Lord's request, "This do in remembrance of Me." The Lord's Supper was to be a memorial and a "showing forth," or declaration, of His death till He returns (1 Cor. 11:23-26).

Roman Catholics teach that in the Lord's Supper the bread and wine become the *actual* body and blood of our Lord, though their appearance remains the same. This view is called *transubstantiation*. They further teach that the body and blood of Christ, are offered every time a mass is observed. Scripture, however, emphatically contradicts such ideas. Christ's death on the cross was a complete and fully effective sacrifice, and He died once for all (Heb. 10:10; cf. 7:27; 9:12).

Lutherans believe in *consubstantiation*. In this view Christ is present *with* the unchanged substance of the bread.

Most Protestants, however, believe either that the elements are only a symbolic memorial or that by faith the believer, in the communion, enters into a special spiritual union with the glorified Christ.

Though participation in neither of these ordinances is necessary for salvation, every true believer should want to show his devotion to Christ by following Him in baptism and by remembering Him in the Lord's Supper.

Each genuine Christian, regardless of denomination, is spiritually one with every other believer. All are in the Church Universal. We are united in Christ, who is our life. There is no such thing as "lone-wolf" Christianity. If we are obedient to our Lord, we will identify with and join other believers for worship and service. In so doing, we not only contribute our own unique gifts to the fellowship, to be used by God to help bless others, but are ourselves blessed.

For Further Reading

Bainton, Roland H. *The Church of Our Fathers* (revised ed.). New York: Charles Scribners, 1950.

Bruce, F. F. *The Spreading Flame*. Grand Rapids: Eerdmans, 1953.

Flew, R. Newton. *Jesus and His Church* (new ed.). Naperville, Ill.: Allenson, 1956.

Latourette, Kenneth S. *Christianity Through the Ages*. New York: Harper, 1965.

Chapter 8

Angels, Satan, and Demons

"Guardian angel" is a common expression, often used quite seriously and sincerely. In San Francisco there is a Church of Satan, with a minister who calls himself a high priest of Satan. Primitive peoples are often dominated by demons.

Are angels, the devil, and demons the result of ignorant superstition, or are they objective realities? The Bible speaks clearly about each of these types of spiritual beings. They can affect a Christian, and he is well advised to understand clearly who and what they are. Otherwise he is in danger of being victimized by popular ideas that may be totally erroneous and harmful.

Angels

Angels are mentioned in both the Old and the New Testaments. Jesus Himself referred to them many times. Speaking about "little ones," Jesus said, "In heaven their angels do always behold the face of My Father" (Matt. 18:10). Concerning His return to earth in the last days, He said, "But of that day and that hour knoweth no man, no, not the angels which are in heaven" (Mark 13:32). Other references He made to angels are recorded in Mark 8:38; Matthew 13:41; 26:53.

Angels are created beings. "For by Him were all things created that are in heaven, and that are in earth, visible and invisible, whether they be thrones, or dominions, or principalities, or powers; all things were created by Him and for Him" (Col. 1:16). Angels probably preceded man in creation; Satan, presumably a fallen angel, visited the Garden of Eden to tempt man. The words, "In the beginning God created the heaven and the earth," probably include the creation of angels, though they are not specifically mentioned.

Unlike man, who is composed of body and spirit, angels are incorporeal (purely spirit) beings. "Are they not all ministering spirits?" (Heb. 1:14) They at times take bodily form, as when two angels came to Lot in Sodom (Gen. 19:1), and sometimes they become visible, as at the Resurrection (John 20:12). Such appearances, however, were exceptions rather than the rule.

Though the masculine gender is always used with the word "angel," there is no distinction of sex with these beings. Jesus referred to this truth when He said of resurrected believers, "They neither marry nor are given in marriage, but are as the angels of God in heaven" (Matt. 22:30).

Angels are eternal; they never die. They are

not subject to aging, and in heaven we shall be like them in this respect. "Neither can [the saved in heaven] die anymore; for they are equal unto the angels" (Luke 20:36).

In God's order of creation, angels are higher than man. God has made man a little lower than the angels (Ps. 8:5). But redeemed man, as part of the new creation, is higher than the angels and will have authority over them. "Know ye not that we shall judge angels?" (1 Cor. 6:3)

The intelligence and power of angels are greater than man's, though they are limited or finite. This truth is implied in our Lord's statement that the angels, though they are in heaven, do not know the day or the hour of the end time (Mark 13:32). The Gospel and salvation are things the angels "desire to look into" (1 Peter 1:12), which implies that they do not fully understand them. Angels are also referred to as greater in power and might than men (2 Peter 2:11). They excel in strength (Ps. 103:20). One angel killed 185,000 Assyrians in one night (Isa. 37:36). The angels' power is not theirs inherently, but comes by delegation from God. The Greek term translated "angel" means, literally, "messenger." Angels are, basically, messengers or servants of God. They are messengers of His might (cf. 2 Thess. 1:7).

Angels stand in the very presence of God. Jesus said they "behold the face of My Father" (Matt. 18:10). They are higher than men in this respect, and they continually worship God (cf. Rev. 5:11, 12; Isa. 6:3). They also take pleasure in His works and grace, and show awareness of and interest in individual human beings. "There is joy in the presence of the angels of God over one sinner that repents" (Luke 15:10).

Angelic Activity

The activity of angels on earth has a number of facets, though essentially it is concerned with the doing of God's will: "Ye His angels . . . that do His commandments . . . that do His pleasure" (Ps. 103:20, 21).

Angels punish the enemies of God and execute His judgment, as Herod discovered when "the angel of the Lord smote him, because he gave not God the glory" (Acts 12:23). God sent an angel to destroy Jerusalem in David's time (1 Chron. 21: 15).

A more comforting truth is the relationship of angels to individual believers. Angels protected Daniel because of his faithfulness to God. To the amazed Darius, who appeared at the lion pit expecting to find him dead, Daniel said, "My God hath sent His angel, and hath shut the lions' mouths, that they have not hurt me" (Dan. 6:22). An angel provided for distraught and hungry Elijah: "An angel touched him and said unto him, 'Arise and eat'" (1 Kings 19:5). Peter was twice released from prison by an angel (Acts 5:19; 12: 8-11). From these instances and others, we see how angels defend, protect, and deliver God's servant when it is in His providence to do so.

Angels may guide Christians to witness to a certain unbeliever, as an angel led Philip to the

Ethiopian (Acts 8:26). Angels may also guide an unbeliever to a Christian, as when Cornelius and Peter were brought together.

In the midst of a shipboard crisis, Paul was cheered by an angel in the night (Acts 27:23). During His agony in the garden, our Lord Himself was strengthened by an angel (Luke 22:43).

Angels are also concerned with the Church and its activity. Paul charged Timothy, concerning his ministry: "Before God and the Lord Jesus Christ and the elect angels . . . observe these things" (1 Tim. 5:21). Women were enjoined to wear veils on their heads "because of the angels" (1 Cor. 11:10), who presumably would be offended by any show of immodesty or indecorum.

Angels will accompany Christ when He comes in glory and in judgment. "The Son of Man shall come . . . and all the holy angels with Him" (Matt. 25:31).

No number of the angels is given in Scripture, but it is clear that they are many. Daniel, of his vision of God, said, "A thousand thousands ministered unto Him, and ten thousand times ten thousand stood before Him" (Dan. 7:10). John reported, of *his* vision, "I heard the voice of many angels round about the throne . . . and the number of them was ten thousand times ten thousand, and thousands of thousands" (Rev. 5:11).

Among this vast number of angels there is organization and rank. Jesus said that had He so desired He could summon more than 12 legions of angels (Matt. 26:53). References to the hosts of heaven in the Old Testament imply organization.

Micaiah said, "I saw the Lord sitting on His throne, and all the host of heaven standing by Him on His right hand and on His left" (1 Kings 22:19).

The statement about "thrones or dominions or principalities or powers" (Col. 1:16) seems to indicate ranking. These orders of heavenly beings are viewed as good, being God-ordained. Evil beings seem to have similar organization and ranking: "principalities . . . powers, . . . the rulers of the darkness of this world, against spiritual wickedness in high places" (Eph. 6:12).

Other Angelic Beings

Michael is the only archangel mentioned in Scripture. He is considered as a special guardian of Israel and as "one of the chief princes" (Dan. 10:13, 21). He contended with the devil for the body of Moses (Jude 9). It may have been Michael who spoke to Moses on Mount Sinai, or Horeb (Ex. 3:2). He led the battle in heaven against Satan (Rev. 12:7).

Apocryphal, Babylonian, and Persian sources mention seven archangels. That only one archangel is mentioned in the Bible indicates that the biblical doctrine of angels was not derived from secular sources, as some critics suggest.

The only other angel named in the Bible is Gabriel, renowned for blowing his horn. Presumably this association comes from 1 Thessalonians 4:16, where Christ's return is said to be accompanied by "the voice of the archangel and the trump of God." Gabriel appears in the Old Testament as the one commissioned to explain the vision of the ram and the he-goat to Daniel (Dan. 8:16) and to declare the prophecy of the 70 weeks (9:21-27). In the New Testament he announced two great births — of John to Zacharias and Elizabeth and of Jesus to Mary (Luke 1:19, 26). Gabriel evidently has high rank as one who continually stands in the very presence of the Lord (Luke 1:19). His function seems to be that of a messenger, while Michael's appears to be that of a warrior.

Angels are never mediators between man and God, and men are not to worship them. Certain ancient Greek philosophers developed a whole series of graded emanations or spirits through which men could make contact with God. These philosophers maintained that God is much too holy to have anything to do with material things in general, and with earth and man in particular. Ancient Zoroastrianism taught a similar belief. This sort of doctrine is totally foreign to the teaching of the Bible, however. Angels are God's messengers, but this in no way implies that He has no direct contact with men when He so chooses. It emphatically is not necessary for us to approach God through any medium other than Jesus Christ.

In most popular thinking and art, angels are winged creatures. There is little biblical warrant for this notion. In Scripture, angels most often appear in manlike form. The only winged beings mentioned in Scripture are cherubim and seraphim (the singular forms are *cherub* and *seraph*). We do not have a great deal of information about either. God stationed cherubim at the east entrance of the Garden of Eden with a flaming sword to guard the tree of life (Gen. 3:24). In Ezekiel's vision (chaps. 1; 10), cherubim are called "living creatures." Each cherub is described as having four faces — of man, lion, ox, and eagle. Each has four wings; two are stretched upward and two downward to cover his body.

Seraphim are mentioned in Isaiah's vision of the heavenly temple. They have six wings and can fly (Isa. 6:2, 6). These beings apparently were human in form, apart from their wings, and were associated with the cherubim in guarding the divine throne. It is possible that the cherubim and seraphim are in some way related to the living creatures in heaven (Rev. 4; 5).

Contrary to a popular mythology, there is absolutely no scriptural warrant for the idea that a person becomes an angel after he dies.

The question often arises as to whether angels appear today as they did in biblical times. Experience does not indicate that such appearances are usual. There is, however, no biblical teaching that rules out this possibility. It would be wise, however, to maintain an attitude of healthy skepticism toward any story of an angelic appearance, unless the report were independently verified. Sometimes impressionable people have hallucinations, and sometimes they embellish their stories unwittingly in retelling them.

"One story about angels which seems to be authentic has to do with the well-known missionary to the New Hebrides, John G. Paton. Since he had aroused the enmity of the local native chief by his successes in the Gospel, the chief hired a man to kill the missionary. The man went to the missionary's house, but instead of murdering Paton he returned in terror, saying he had seen a row of men, dressed in white, surrounding the missionary's home. The chief thought the man had drunk too much whiskey and encouraged him to try again. The next time others of the tribe accompanied him. That night they all saw *three* rows of men surrounding Paton's home.

"When the Chief asked the missionary where he kept the men in the daytime who surrounded his house at night, Paton, knowing nothing of what had happened, disclaimed the whole idea. When the Chief, in amazement, told his story, the missionary realized the natives had seen an angelic company which God had sent to protect him, and he related it to Psalm 34:7: 'The angel of the Lord encampeth round about them that fear Him, and delivereth them.' The savages were powerfully impressed with the missionary's explanation, as well they might be."⁴⁶

Evil Spiritual Beings

God created angels perfect, and they were originally uncorrupted in spirit. At the same time, they had free will and were susceptible to temptation and sin. How sin could have come into the experience of a perfect creature is a mystery, but that it actually happened is clear. Peter warns against apostasy on the basis of God's judgment on angels (2 Peter 2:4), and we read of angels that "kept not their first estate, but left their own habitation" (Jude 6). Some feel that this angelic fall took place after the Creation (Gen. 1:1) and that because of it the original creation became "without form and void" (v. 2). The cause of the angels' fall is not specified, but presumably is related to the fall of Satan.

The name *Satan* means "adversary" or opponent. Peter calls him "your adversary the devil" (1 Peter 5:8). Joshua stood before the angel of the Lord, with "Satan standing at his right hand to resist him" (Zech. 3:1). Satan ("adversary") is the opposer and enemy of both God and His people.

It has been fashionable, in recent years, to consider belief in the existence and personality of Satan as primitive, naive, and even superstitious. It is suggested instead that Satan, if we must use the term, is only the personification of the evil in the world. This notion has resulted partly from reaction to extravagant ideas and poetic expressions about Satan that were prominent during the Middle Ages. But these distorted ideas have no basis in Scripture, our only source of authoritative information.

Nowhere does the Bible depict Satan as a red man with horns, a tail, and a pitchfork. Some suggest that these caricatures are part of Satan's wiles to persuade sophisticated Twentieth Century men that he doesn't exist. People's credulity makes his job that much less difficult.

Biblically, there can be no doubt as to the devil's existence and personality. He is presented as appearing before the Lord when God challenged

146

him about Job (Job 1:6-12; 2:1-7). There is no mistaking Satan's reality in his temptation of our Lord in the wilderness. He spoke to Jesus and Jesus spoke to him (Matt. 4:1-11).

Satan's Other Names

Satan's other scriptural names also indicate his reality and personality. The only other proper name given him is *Devil*. Other terms applied to him describe him and his work. He is *the tempter*: (1 Thes. 3:5). He is the *wicked one* who snatches away the good seed of the Word of God out of people's hearts (Matt. 13:19). He is the *enemy* who sows tares among the good seed (Matt. 13:39). He is our *adversary* (1 Peter 5:8). Jesus calls him the *father of lies* and a *murderer* (John 8:44). He is the supreme *deceiver* (Rev. 12:9).

Belial (2 Cor. 6:15) and *Beelzebub* (Matt. 12:24) have obscure derivations, but are used as synonyms for Satan. They denote a wicked person.

The fall of Satan from his exalted position as a perfect angel is shrouded in mystery, as is that of the other angels who fell with him. Presumably they shared his attitudes and he became their leader. Many Bible students feel that two Old Testament passages give clues as to what led to Satan's rebellion and fall.

One of these passages is Ezekiel 28:12-19. Though the entire passage speaks of the "prince of Tyrus" (v. 12), it seems also to characterize a being who was more than a mere man. What is said of Tyrus could only be applied to the earthly king of Tyre in a graphic and figurative sense. But if we take what is said as applying to Satan, we learn that he was, as originally created, "full of wisdom and perfect in beauty" (v. 12). The passage also indicates that originally he was assigned by God to the earth. The statement, "Thou wast perfect in thy ways from the day that thou was created till iniquity wast found in thee," would indicate that though he was created perfect, he *became* sinful. Since this sin dates back to pre-Adamic times, Satan probably was the originator of sin. His sin was pride.

The second of the two passages is Isaiah 14: 12-15, which, if we take it to refer to Satan, describes the nature of his initial sin. The passage refers specifically to the King of Babylon, but there are reasons for believing that Satan wants to identify with the leading political power in the world at any given period of history. If this is so, it is easy to see how he may be described as the King of Tyre at one time and as the King of Babylon at another. The Lord Jesus three times referred to him as "the prince of this world" (John 12:31; 14:30; 17:11). Scripture teaches that the affairs of nations and cultures are affected by both angels and demons.

If Isaiah 14 refers to Satan, we see that he may have felt that his assignment on earth was too trivial for his status, which may well have been that of archangel. He is called "Lucifer, son of the morning" (Isa. 14:12). The word Lucifer means "shining one," or "light bearer." As a created being and a servant of God, he perhaps was not fully aware of his Master's plan concerning the earth (cf. John 15:15), and therefore did not understand its importance as the sphere where God would display Himself both in His creature, man, and later in the incarnation of His Son.

In the five "I wills" attributed to Satan (Isa. 14:13, 14), some see the root of all sin — the setting of a creature's mind and will against God's. In the Garden of Eden, Satan cast doubts on God's love and wisdom (Gen. 3:4, 5), as though God either did not know what was best for man or was unwilling to give it to him. "God's will is always the highest good His wisdom can devise. In the Garden of Eden Satan succeeded in convincing man that he could do better for himself than God had planned for him; and this is a contemporary problem in the world today."[47]

There are similarities between the description in Isaiah, Jesus' statement ("I beheld Satan as lightning fall from heaven," Luke 10:18), and the vision of John on Patmos: "I saw a star fall from heaven unto the earth: and to him was given the key of the bottomless pit" (Rev. 9:1). These passages all refer to Satan and they further indicate his identification with Lucifer.

After being cast out of heaven, Satan continued his work of opposition to God in the Garden of Eden, where he succeeded in tempting Adam and Eve to sin. He has continued his diabolical work through man's history, and is actively prosecuting it to this day. He is "the god of this world, [who] hath blinded the minds of them that believe not" (2 Cor. 4:4). This is an important fact to remember in evangelism, which is not merely a contest of human wills or intellects. The opponent of Christian witness is "the *prince of the power of the air,* the spirit that now worketh in the children of disobedience" (Eph. 2:2). He heads a powerful kingdom whose earthly subjects only Christ can turn "from darkness to light and from the power of Satan unto God" (Acts 26:18).

Our Lord was accused of casting out demons by the power of "the prince of demons" (Matt. 9:34, asv). Demons are most likely fallen angels. They carry out the same kinds of activity as Satan.

Demon Possession

In modern times, many theologians regard demon possession as only a primitive, prescientific description of what we now call mental illness. Throughout history, undoubtedly, some victims of mental illness have been wrongly accused of demon possession, and so treated harshly. But we should guard against confusion of the two conditions.

Some people suggest that all sickness is initiated and caused by demons, but the New Testament makes clear distinctions: "They brought to [Jesus] all who were ill, taken with various diseases and pains, demoniacs, epileptics, paralytics" (Matt. 4:24, nas). Here clear differentiation is made between ordinary diseases and demon possession, and between demon possession and lunacy.

On another occasion Jesus cast out a demon who had caused dumbness (Matt. 9:32, 33). From this account it is clear that the results of demon possession are not exclusively mental or nervous. Nor does the Bible connect epilepsy and demon possession. The boy Jesus healed of fits (Matt. 17: 15-18) seems to have been afflicted with more than epilepsy. The Gadarene maniac (Mark 5: 1-20), and possibly the man who overpowered two sons of the exorcist, Sceva (Acts 19:16), in addition to being demon possessed, may also have been afflicted with mental illness.

Demon possession is seldom mentioned in the Old Testament, The Acts, or the epistles. The incidents of it centered around our Lord's ministry and may indicate a special attack on mankind by Satan during that period.

Demon possession is a worldwide phenomenon, however, with authenticated contemporary cases being reported in this country as well as in other parts of the world. It is apparently possible deliberately to open oneself to demons. Trifling with the occult or playing around the edges of the spirit world are dangerous practices and Christians should carefully avoid them.

We should never try to conquer demons by our own power. Even the disciples had some frustrating encounters with such spirits. Jesus said, "This kind can come forth by nothing but prayer and fasting" (Mark 9:29). Generally, evil spirits were exorcised by being commanded to come out in the name of Christ (e.g., Acts 16:18). It has been suggested that rather than attempt to exorcise a satanic spirit ourselves, even in the name of

Christ, we should ask God to do so for us. Even Michael the archangel did this (Jude 9).

A demon-possessed person invariably acts in ways that are not natural and normal to him. He often speaks in a voice entirely different from his normal one, and sometimes displays superhuman strength. He may also have powers of telepathy and clairvoyance. It should be noted that possession, in every instance, is by demons or evil spirits, never by good spirits.

Despite the great power of Satan and his demons, however, a Christian need not fear them if he is in close fellowship with the Lord. The Holy Spirit's presence in us is a reality and insures our safety (1 John 4:4).

These truths are clear from scriptural teachings and their implications about Satan and demons.
. First, Satan's power over a believer is limited. The devil could not touch Job without God's permission (Job 1:9-12; 2:4-6). Demons had to ask permission of Christ to enter swine (Mark 5:12). Satan is *not* all-powerful.

Neither is the devil all-knowing. If he were, he would have known in advance the futility of his scheme to subvert Job, and he would surely have realized that it was useless for him to tempt the Lord in the wilderness.

Satan was conquered by Christ on the Cross. There, "having spoiled principalities and powers, He made a show of them openly, triumphing over them in it" (Col. 2:15). We are told that "for this purpose the Son of God was manifested, that He might destroy the works of the devil" (1 John 3:8).

Satan is slated for final eternal judgment: "And the devil that deceived them was cast into the lake of fire and brimstone, where the beast and the false prophet are, and shall be tormented day and night forever and ever" (Rev. 20:10).

Because Satan has been overcome by Christ, Christians are encouraged by God's promise that if they resist the devil he will flee from them (James 4:7). But our resistance must be "steadfast in the faith" (1 Peter 5:9). We can best thwart Satan's designs on us by daily yielding ourselves to the Lord in prayer and by putting on the whole armor of God (Eph. 6:10-17).

We should avoid the extreme of trying to see Satan behind every misfortune, in this way evading our personal responsibility. Equally dangerous, however, is being so lulled by the sophistication of our age as to be unaware of Satan and his wiles against us in the spiritual battle in which every true believer is engaged.

For Further Reading

Koch, Kurt. *Christian Counseling and Occultism*. Grand Rapids: Kregel, 1965.

Lewis, C. S. *Screwtape Letters*. New York: Macmillan, 1947.

Peterson, Robert. *The Roaring Lion*. London: Overseas Missionary Fellowship, 1968.

Unger, Merrill F. *Biblical Demonology*. Wheaton, Ill.: Scripture Press, 1952.

Chapter 9

Salvation

From one point of view, salvation is very simple. It can be summed up in Paul's words to the Philippian jailer: "Believe on the Lord Jesus Christ and thou shalt be saved" (Acts 16:31). At the same time, salvation is profound; it has the most pervasive and permanent impact possible on the one who experiences it. We do not, of course, have to understand all the aspects of salvation before we can receive it. We may understand very little when we first trust Christ. A great deal we will not understand until we see our Lord face to face. But studying God's Word and trying to understand more fully the truth of our salvation greatly enriches us spiritually.

Several theological terms are generally used in connection with salvation. Each contributes something and, taken together, they give a greater fullness of God's light. None of these terms or truths can be isolated completely from the others. We should always study them in context. We cannot always be dogmatic about the order, or sequence, in which an individual should experience these various aspects of salvation, for they often overlap and sometimes are simply different views of the same truth.

Repentance

John the Baptist began his ministry with a call to *repentance*: "Repent ye, for the kingdom of heaven is at hand" (Matt. 3:2). Jesus began preaching with the identical words (Matt. 4:17). He commanded His disciples that "repentance and remission of sins should be preached in His name among all nations, beginning at Jerusalem" (Luke 24:47). Peter took up this message on the Day of Pentecost (Acts 2:38). Paul points out that now God "commandeth all men everywhere to repent" (Acts 17:30, cf. 26:20). Acceptance of the Gospel, to both Jews and Greeks, consists of "repentance toward God, and faith toward our Lord Jesus Christ" (Acts 20:21).

The word used in the Old Testament for repentance means to turn or return. It implies a personal decision to turn away from sin and *to* God. In the New Testament, the terms "repent" and "repentance" that apply to man's relationship to sin and God have the basic meaning of a change of mind. They imply a change of mind about sin, and a turning to God. In a sense, they are the negative and positive aspects of the same truth. The two together are inseparable and complementary. Paul, in his defense before Agrippa, said he preached that both Jews and Gentiles "should repent and turn to God and do works meet for repentance" (Acts 26:20).

True repentance is not merely a feeling of remorse, such as Judas had after he betrayed the Lord. It involves the intellect, the emotions, and the will.

Repentance brings the mind to realize both the holiness of God's law and one's utter failure and inability to keep it. It may also involve a change of mind as to who Christ is, as was true with the Jews on the Day of Pentecost (Acts 2:14-40). They had formerly viewed Jesus as an imposter, but Peter called on them to accept Him as Messiah and Saviour.

The emotions are involved in repentance. "Godly sorrow," in contrast to one's being superficially sorry for sin, often precedes the change of mind. "The sadness that is used by God brings a change of heart that leads to salvation — and there is no regret in that!" (2 Cor. 7:10, TEV). Repentance involves a feeling of the awfulness of sin in its effect on man and his relationship to God. Emotion, however, is no gauge of the extent of one's repentance. The presence or absence of tears does not necessarily indicate genuineness or lack of it. But when we truly repent we are sure to experience some feeling about it.

Repentance involves the will. The prodigal son not only came to his senses intellectually, and felt a loathing for himself and what he had done, but he *acted*: "I will arise and go to my father. . . .

And he arose" (Luke 15:18, 20). Repentance is deliberate, willful turning away from sin and following after God. True repentance *always* leads to a change in conduct or attitude.

Faith

Repentance, if it is genuine, will lead to *faith*. In fact, some Christians understand "faith" to *include* repentance, pointing out that for a person to receive Christ as his Saviour in faith is in itself evidence that he is aware of his need, as a sinner, for the Saviour. The term *faith*, in its noun, verb, and adjective forms, is used dozens of times in the Old Testament, but occurs several hundred times in the New Testament. Its most common meaning is confident trust in or reliance on.

Faith is central to the whole Christian experience. "Without faith it is impossible to please [God], for he that cometh to [Him] must believe that He is, and that He is a rewarder of them that diligently seek Him" (Heb. 11:6). Faith, in the New Testament, always has as its background the Person and work of Christ. He is the object of our faith, reliance, or trust. Whoever believes in Him will not perish, but has everlasting life (John 3:16). In and of itself, faith is meaningless. It always has an object to which it is directed and upon which it rests. If the object of our faith is worthless, we are a victim of superstition, no matter how intensely and sincerely we believe.

Saving faith consists of several elements. First are the *facts* about Christ — His Deity, His death, and our need of Him. We must accept these facts as *true*, though mere mental assent to this truth does not save us. James makes this clear: "Thou believest there is one God; thou doest well; the demons also believe and tremble" (James 2:19, ASV). One could not possibly be a Christian without believing these basic facts, but saving faith goes beyond mere belief *about* Christ to complete commitment *to* and trust *in* Him. Such commitment involves the *will* as well as the mind and the emotions. One does not believe simply because of one's feelings — one *decides* to believe.

Faith is the instrument that links us to Christ. The New Testament emphasizes that we are saved by *faith* and not by *works*. "But to him that worketh not, but believeth on Him that justifieth the ungodly, his faith is counted for righteousness" (Rom. 4:5).

At first sight, the Epistle of James appears to disagree: "What doth it profit, my brethren, though a man say he hath faith and have not works. Can [such] faith save him? . . . Ye see, then, how that by works a man is justified, and not by faith only" (James 2:14, 24).

The "faith" James criticizes is "head belief" — mere intellectual assent to facts. Such "faith" does not lead to holy living and hence is worthless, or "dead" (James 2:20). It has no saving value. When we read about "faith" in the other epistles, wholehearted trust in Christ is in view. This is the faith on the basis of which God credits a believer with righteousness and which leads its possessor to want a holy life.

When we read that we are saved by faith rather than by "works," the works in view are the keeping of the Law in an effort to earn salvation. James (2:14, 18, 20) does not use the term "works" in this sense. His "works" are very much like "the fruit of the Spirit" of which Paul speaks (Gal. 5: 22). "They are warm deeds of love springing from a right attitude to God. They are the fruits of faith. What James objects to is the claim that faith is there when there is no fruit to attest it."[48]

How does faith come about? "Faith cometh by hearing, and hearing by the Word of God" (Rom. 10:17). In the days of the apostles, "many of [the people] who heard the Word believed" (Acts 4: 4). God uses His Word, both spoken and written, to produce faith. At the same time, "God hath dealt to every man the measure of faith" (Rom. 12:3), which implies that faith is a work of God.

In almost every phase of salvation there is a mysterious interplay between the divine and human sides. It is not always possible, though, to draw neat lines of distinction. For instance, we may think of *repentance* and *faith* as man's response to *regeneration,* which God produces.

Regeneration

"Regeneration, or the new birth, is the divine side of that change of heart which, viewed from the human side, we call conversion."[49] The term is used only twice in the New Testament — of the restoration of the world (Matt. 19:28) and of the renewal or rebirth of individuals: "Not by works of righteousness which we have done, but according to His mercy He saved us, by the washing of regeneration and renewing of the Holy Spirit" (Titus 3:5).

Sin is so serious that a sinner cannot even *see* the kingdom of God, let alone *enter* it, unless he is born from above, or born again (John 3:3) — as Jesus pointed out in His conversation with the Jewish leader, Nicodemus. God takes the initiative in regeneration, or rebirth, but man must actively respond in faith. "But as many as received Him, to them gave He power to become the sons of God, even to them that believe on His name, which were born not of blood, nor of the will of the flesh, nor of the will of man, but of God" (John 1:12, 13). "God, who is rich in mercy . . . even when we were dead in sins, hath quickened us together with Christ" (Eph. 2:4, 5).

The new birth results not in a change of personality as such, but in a whole new way of life. Before the new birth, self and sin are in control; but after it, the Holy Spirit is in control. A born-again person shares in the very life of God. He becomes a "partaker of the divine nature" (2 Peter 1:4), and is described as a "new creation" (1 Cor. 5:17, ASV); he puts on "the new man, which after God is created in righteousness and holiness" (Eph. 4:24; cf. Col. 3:10). Regeneration is a decisive experience that happens once for all, though it has continuing results in the life of a Christian.

God wants "all men to be saved and come to a knowledge of the truth" (1 Tim. 2:4). That some men are not regenerated or reborn is not God's fault. The responsibility rests with men. Our Lord diagnosed this problem. When speaking to a typical group, He said, "Ye *will not* come to Me that ye might have life" (John 5:40). It wasn't that they *could* not have come, but that they *would* not. They deliberately refused.

How men actually come to faith in Christ is a profound question. Some, by approaching the problem entirely from man's side, have tended to eclipse the sovereignty of God. Others, by approaching it only from God's side, have seemed to obliterate man's freedom.

We need to understand several theological terms to avoid confusion and popular misconceptions. These terms are election, predestination, and foreknowledge.

Election

Election has to do with God's choice of certain groups and people to receive His grace. This choice is based on His sovereign pleasure and not on the value, goodness, or disposition of those chosen. In the Old Testament, God's election is illustrated in His choice of Abraham, with whom He made an everlasting covenant, and of Abraham's descendants, the nation of Israel, to have a special relationship with Himself (Gen. 11:31–12:7).

Election, as used in the New Testament, has to do with God's choice of particular individuals for salvation. Jesus said, "And then shall [God] send His angels and shall gather together His elect [chosen] from the four winds" (Mark 13:27).

Christians are "elect [chosen] according to the foreknowledge of God the Father" (1 Peter 1:2). God has "chosen [elected] us in Him before the foundation of the world . . . having predestinated us unto the adoption of children by Jesus Christ to Himself according to the good pleasure of His will" (Eph. 1:4, 5). Jesus Himself explicitly said, "Ye have not chosen Me, but I have chosen [elected] you and ordained you" (John 15:16).

Predestination and Foreknowledge

Closely allied to election are *predestination* and *foreknowledge.* Predestination is a term used only of Christians. It indicates that God's purpose for a believer — that he become Christlike — is sure to be fulfilled. "For whom He did foreknow, He also did predestinate to be conformed to the image of His Son. . . . Moreover, whom He did predestinate, them He also called; and whom He called, them He also justified, and whom He justified, them He also glorified" (Rom. 8:29, 30). Foreknowledge, predestination, calling, justification, and glorification are all grouped together in one "package." A person who has *one* of them has them *all.* The sequence indicates that apart from the grace of God we cannot trust in Christ. Jesus said, "No man can come to Me except the Father that sent Me draw him" (John 6:44).

Like election, *predestination* is according to God's sovereign purpose and will. It is not based on any merits in those persons whom He has chosen.

162

It is important to realize that *all* men are sinners and are under the judgment of God. "God in sovereign freedom treats some sinners as they deserve . . . but He selects others to be 'vessels of mercy,' receiving the 'riches of His glory' (Rom. 9:23). This discrimination involves no injustice, for the Creator owes mercy to none and has a right to do as He pleases with His rebellious creatures (Rom. 9:14-21). The wonder is not that He withholds mercy from some, but that He should be gracious to any."[50]

The purpose of the Bible's teaching on election and predestination is to lead pardoned sinners to worship God for the grace they have experienced. They come to see, in unmistakable terms, that salvation is *all* of God and not at all of themselves. They also come to see that since they were chosen in Christ before the foundation of the world, their election is eternal and therefore certain. This inspires devotion and love to Christ in gratitude for God's unfathomable love.

The popular misconception of election and predestination as the arbitrary acts of a capricious tyrant is totally foreign and unfair to Scripture. The attitude often expressed by unbelievers is that if they are elect, they'll get into heaven anyway, and if they're not, there's no use in their trying. In either case, they reason, they needn't be concerned. This is a tragic misconception. No one in hell will be able to tell God, "I wanted to be saved, but my name was on the wrong list."

Election and predestination are always to salvation and its blessings — never to judgment. It is true that no one believes on the Saviour unless God the Holy Spirit convicts him, but it is also true that those who do not trust Christ *choose* not to believe. God never refuses to save anyone who wants salvation.

Some feel that the expression, "elect according to the foreknowledge of God" (1 Peter 1:2) means that God elects to salvation those whom He knows in advance will respond positively to the Gospel. But foreknowledge is not the same thing as fore-ordination or election.

Throughout Church History, honest differences of opinion have arisen about these complex and not fully explainable doctrines. Each believer should be persuaded in his own mind about them, and should show a charitable spirit toward those who differ with him.

A conversation between Charles Simeon and John Wesley, on Dec. 20, 1874, is helpful at this point. Simeon said, "Sir, I understand that you are called an Arminian; and I have sometimes been called a Calvinist; and therefore I suppose we are to draw draggers. But before I consent to begin the combat, with your permission, I will ask you a few questions. . . . Pray, Sir, do you feel yourself a depraved creature, so depraved that you would never have thought of turning to God if God had not first put it in your heart?"

"Yes," said Wesley, "I do indeed."

"And do you utterly despair of recommending yourself to God by anything you can do, and look for salvation solely through the blood and righteousness of Christ?"

"Yes, solely through Christ."

"But, Sir, supposing you were at first saved by Christ, are you not somehow or other to save yourself afterwards by your own works?"

"No, I must be saved by Christ from first to last."

"Allowing, then, that you were first turned by the grace of God, are you not in some way or other to keep yourself by your own power?"

"No."

"What then? Are you to be upheld every hour and every moment by God, as much as an infant in its mother's arms?"

"Yes, altogether."

"And is all your hope in the grace and mercy of God to preserve you unto His heavenly kingdom?"

"Yes, I have no hope but in Him."

"Then, Sir, with your leave I will put up my dagger again; for this is all my Calvinism; this is my election, my justification by faith, my final perseverance: it is in substance all that I hold, and as I hold it; and therefore, if you please, instead of searching out terms and phrases to be a ground of contention between us, we will cordially unite in those things wherein we agree."[51]

The experience of salvation, in relation to the divine and human factors, includes some ambiguities. The results of salvation, however, are very clear. There are three phases of salvation: past, present, and future. That we have *been* saved, that we are *being* saved, and we *shall* be saved are all true statements. Each refers to a particular aspect of salvation.

Justification

Justification has often been defined as meaning, "Just as if I'd never sinned." This aspect involves acquittal, but justification goes even farther by declaring a person to be *righteous*. When God justifies us, He does not merely forgive our sins, making us neutral — moral and spiritual ciphers. He sees us in Christ as having His perfect righteousness. Justification has to do with our standing before God, and is *objective*. It does not make one *personally* righteous, but it *declares* him righteous in a legal sense, and brings him into right relationship with God.

Paul, to whom justification is central in salvation, stresses that we cannot be justified by the works of the Law, "for by the Law is the knowledge of sin" (Rom. 3:20). Rather, we are "justified freely by [God's] grace through the redemption that is in Christ Jesus" (Rom. 3:24).

The *basis*, or ground, of our justification, or being declared righteous, is twofold. Christ's death as our Substitute satisfied the claims of God's holy law against our sin. "While we were yet sinners, Christ died for us. Much more then, being now justified by His blood, we shall be saved from wrath through Him" (Rom. 5:8, 9).

The other basis of God's declaring us righteous is Christ's perfect obedience. "For as by one man's [Adam's] disobedience many [i.e., all men] were made sinners, so by the obedience of One [Christ] shall many [i.e., all who believe] be made righteous" (Rom. 5:19). Christ became identified with us when He was made sin for us on the cross; and we are identified with Him in His newness of resurrection life, and share His righteousness.

We are justified by faith. This truth burst upon the heart and mind of Martin Luther like a bombshell as he considered the words: "Therefore being justified by faith, we have peace with God through our Lord Jesus Christ" (Rom. 5:1). After long struggling in unsuccessful self-effort to win the favor of God, Luther suddenly realized it was not what *he* could do, but what *God* had done, that made justification and peace possible. The Protestant Reformation resulted from this discovery.

The fact that we have been justified becomes clear through the evidence of our changed lives, marked by obedience to God and desire to do His will. When we say that we *have been* saved, we are referring to our justification. Paul wrote to the Ephesians, "For by grace are ye saved through faith" (Eph. 2:8). Paul's certainty of a past event, based on what God has done, led him to overflow with assurance. "I am persuaded," he wrote, "that neither death, nor life, nor angels, nor principalities, nor powers, nor things present, nor things to come, . . . nor any other creature shall be able to separate us from the love of God which is in Christ Jesus our Lord" (Rom. 8:38, 39). We, too, may enjoy such assurance, for our salvation is an accomplished fact if we are in Christ.

Sanctification

But we are also *being* saved. This process of becoming holy is called *sanctification*. Justification

167

has to do with our standing before God and is instantaneous. Sanctification has to do with our character and conduct and is progressive. It continues as long as we live.

Basically, the word "sanctified" means "set apart." The term "saint" comes from the same root and means "a set-apart one." Another word with the same meaning is "holy."

"Sanctify" is used in two ways:

(1) To set apart, or declare holy, for God's use or service. Christians are called "saints" in this sense — God has set them apart for His service. Such "sanctification" is usually regarded as being instantaneous and as taking place at the time of one's conversion. "Ye are washed . . . ye are sanctified . . . ye are justified in the name of the Lord Jesus and by the Spirit of God" (1 Cor. 6:11).

(2) To make the personal life of an individual Christian holy, in the sense of moral and spiritual improvement. This is a lifelong process. We are to "grow in grace and in the knowledge of . . . Jesus Christ" (2 Peter 3:18), and as we mature spiritually we "are changed into the same image [that of Christ] from glory to glory, even as by the Spirit of the Lord" (2 Cor. 3:18).

Some feel that sanctification is a crisis experience, as is justification, and that one can experience "entire sanctification" in a moment of time. Differences of opinion on this question hinge almost completely on the definition of sin and on the standard of holy living meant. Sin is often defined as "any voluntary transgression of a known law," as Wesley put it. The Westminster Shorter

Catechism, on the other hand, defines sin as "any want of conformity unto or transgression of the law of God." This definition includes sins of omission and also takes our sinful nature into consideration — as well as overt sins committed deliberately.

Another big question has to do with *how* God sanctifies us. Those who say the process is all of God tend to minimize human responsibility. On the other hand, those who tend to minimize sin exaggerate human responsibility in sanctification.

A key principle that recognizes both God's initiative and man's responsibility is expressed in the scriptural command, "Work out your own salvation with fear and trembling. For it is God who worketh in you both to will and to do of His good pleasure" (Phil. 2:12, 13). It is because God works in him that man is able to work. On the other hand, although God enables, man must respond. He is to show neither supine passivity nor naive confidence in his own effort.

Justification, declaring us righteous, delivers us from the *penalty* of sin. Sanctification, involving the development of holiness of character, delivers us from the *power* of sin. But how does holiness become *real* in our daily experience? Paul portrays the personal struggle vividly (Rom. 7) and also gives the remedy for it. He says that Christ died so "that the righteousness of the Law might be fulfilled in us, who walk [live] not after the flesh, but after the Spirit" (Rom. 8:4). God's command is, "Walk [live] in the Spirit and ye shall not fulfill the lust of the flesh" (Gal. 5:16). The

Holy Spirit gives us power to overcome sin and produces in us the fruit of the Spirit (Gal. 5:22, 23). This "walk" is a life of daily faith in which we claim and live personally what has already been given us by God. Christ has been made to us "wisdom, righteousness, sanctification, and redemption" (1 Cor. 1:30).

As we depend on Christ, then, His patience, love, power, purity, etc., will begin to show in our attitudes and conduct. He does not dole out these qualities to us in "little packages" — we have all of them we need in Christ, who indwells us. "His divine power has given unto us *all things* that pertain to life and *godliness,* through the knowledge of Him that hath called us to glory and virtue" (2 Peter 1:3).

The key principle in sanctification, as in justification, is faith. We can be *saved* only by faith and we can *live effectively* as Christians only by faith. "As ye have therefore received Christ Jesus the Lord [by faith], so walk [live] ye in him" (Col. 2:6). God, in both instances, does what we cannot do. Our part is to respond in faith.

Glorification

But there is a sense in which salvation is also future: we *shall* be saved. We have been saved from the *penalty* of sin, we are being saved from the *power* of sin, and we shall be saved from the very *presence* of sin. We shall personally be perfect and free from all sin. "Beloved, now are we the sons of God, and it doth not yet appear what we shall be; but we know that when He shall appear, we shall be like Him, for we shall see Him as He is" (1 John 3:2). It is in this sense that we are appointed "to *obtain* salvation" (1 Thes. 5:9), and it is *this* salvation which is ready to be revealed in the last time and to which Paul refers when he says, "Now is our salvation nearer than when we [first] believed" (Rom. 13:11). This complete and final sanctification and deliverance from the very presence of sin are called *glorification*.

Salvation is God's great gift to man. Though in experience its aspects may not be separated, an understanding of its details gives a Christian deeper appreciation, greater love, and happier praise for the God who has saved him.

For Further Reading

Berkouwer, G. C. *Faith and Perseverance*. Grand Rapids: Eerdman, 1958.

Macon, Leon M. *Salvation in a Scientific Age*. Grand Rapids: Zondervan, 1955.

Prior, K. F. W. *The Way of Holiness*. Chicago: Inter-Varsity Press, 1967.

Chapter 10

Things to Come

One of the most fascinating features of the Bible is that it tells what is ahead. Both Old and New Testaments contend that history is moving to a climax and that the sovereign God is in control. Helmut Thielecke, in his book, *The Waiting Father,* sums up this truth in a magnificent way: "When the drama of history is over, Jesus Christ will stand alone upon the stage. All the great figures of history — Pharaoh, Alexander the Great, Charlemagne, Churchill, Stalin, Johnson, Mao Tze Tung — will realize they have been bit actors in a drama produced by Another."[52]

Throughout the Old Testament, the prophets looked forward to "the Day of the Lord," the time when God would exercise final judgment on Israel and other nations for their wickedness. All judgments — whether by means of invasion, plague, or natural disaster — will come to full flower at the return of Christ.

The Old Testament contains two lines of messianic prophecy. One pictures the Messiah (Christ) as the Suffering Servant (e.g., Isa. 53). The other regards Him as a reigning King (e.g., Isa. 9:6). The first coming of Christ, as the Suffering Servant, answered the hope for God's coming to redeem His people. The second coming of Christ will bring consummation of that hope when He returns as reigning King.

In the meantime, though, Satan has been conquered by Christ — at the Cross and in the Resurrection — so that "through death He might destroy him who had the power of death, that is, the devil" (Heb. 2:14). But Satan is, temporarily, still "the god of this world" (2 Cor. 4:4), and he is actively opposing Christ and His Church.

The Antichrist

Satan's opposition will culminate in the appearance of a being called Antichrist. The "spirit of Antichrist" is to be abroad before this person appears. In fact, his presence was noted already in apostolic times: "Little children, it is the last time; and as ye have heard that Antichrist shall come, even now are there many antichrists; whereby we know it is the last time" (1 John 2:18). Of this coming being it is asked, "Who is a liar but he that denieth that Jesus is the Christ? He is Antichrist that denieth the Father and the Son" (v. 22).

Though there is considerable difference of opinion among Bible scholars, some feel, because of the similarity of description given in Daniel 11:37 and

173

2 Thessalonians 2:4, that these passages refer to
the same person. If these also refer to the same
person as "the beast" (Rev. 13:3, 13, 16, 17), several striking characteristics emerge. Satan, with a
view to deceiving and persuading men, will in-
spire Antichrist and give him power to act supernaturally. As an ecclesiastical leader, he will ma-
nipulate religion for his own ends, so as to claim
the worship due God. He will also demand political allegiance and will exercise economic pressure
to force compliance (Rev. 13:16, 17). Those who
try to oppose him will face tribulation so great
that unless God shortened the days no one would
survive (Matt. 24:22, 23).

Christ's Return

The coming of Christ will bring the rule of
Antichrist to an end. It is the great event to which
all Scripture looks forward. The Old Testament
prophets spoke of it, though the first and second
comings often merged in their thinking. Jesus Himself frequently referred to it: "I will come again
and receive you unto Myself, that where I am,
there you may be also" (John 14:3); and, "Immediately after the tribulation of those days . . . shall
appear the sign of the Son of Man in heaven. . . .
And they shall see the Son of Man coming in the
clouds of heaven with power and great glory"
Matt. 24:29, 30). As the disciples watched Jesus'
ascension: "Two men stood by them in white ap-
parel, which also said, 'Ye men of Galilee, why
stand ye gazing up into heaven? This same Jesus

. . . shall so come in like manner as ye have seen Him go into heaven'" (Acts 1:10, 11). The epistles also emphasize it: "For the Lord Himself will descend from heaven with a shout, with the voice of the archangel, and with the trump of God; and the dead in Christ shall rise first" (1 Thes. 4:16).

The second coming of Christ is the great anticipation of the Church. As Christians we should, with Paul, love to look for that "blessed hope and the glorious appearing of the great God and our Saviour Jesus Christ" (Titus 2:13). His coming is an incentive for holy living: "And now, little children, abide in Him; that when He shall appear we may have confidence, and not be ashamed before Him at His coming"; and, "Every man that hath this hope in Him purifieth himself even as He is pure" (1 John 2:28; 3:3).

Views of the Rapture

Bible scholars are not completely agreed as to whether the Second Coming is a single event or has two phases. Many evangelicals distinguish between Christ's coming *for* His saints in the "Rapture" and His coming *with* His saints in the revelation of His power.

Among premillennialists (who believe Christ will return *before* He reigns with His resurrected saints for a thousand years), there are three views, commonly known as the pre-, mid-, and posttribulation views of the Rapture.

Those who hold the pretribulation view believe

that Christ will return *for* His Church *before* the Great Tribulation, which, therefore, believers will not have to endure. After this period of turmoil and affliction on earth, Christ will return again *with* His Church. He will rule as King during the Millennium. The Tribulation, it is believed, coincides with the 70th "week" mentioned in Daniel's prophecy: "And he [the prince that is to come, or Antichrist] shall confirm the covenant with many [i.e., with Israel] for one week; and in the midst of the week he shall cause the sacrifice and the oblation [in the temple at Jerusalem] to cease, and for the overspreading of abomination he shall make it desolate even until the consummation shall be poured upon the desolate" (Dan. 9:27; cf. v. 26).

By comparing the whole prophecy (Dan. 9) with parallel passages, it appears these "weeks" are "sevens" of *years*, not *days*. According to pretribulation interpretation, therefore, the Tribulation will be a literal seven-year period, ruled by Antichrist, just before his final defeat by Christ. Emphasis is laid, in the pre-tribulation Rapture view, on the fact that though the Church, through the centuries, has known much persecution, the final Great Tribulation will not involve believers and will be unique in its awfulness (Matt. 24:21).

The midtribulation view holds that the Rapture will take place in the *middle* of the 70th "week," 3-½ years after its beginning. The posttribulation view is held by premillenarians who believe that Christ's rapture (coming *for* His saints) and His revelation (coming *with* His saints) are one and the same event, occurring just *after* the Tribulation and just before the Millennium.

Is anything yet to happen before Christ can return for His own? Those holding the pretribulation view feel there is nothing to prevent the Rapture from happening at "any moment." This "perhaps today" awareness encourages many Christians as they try to live each day in the light of their Lord's imminent return. Most of those having mid- or posttribulation convictions believe, of course, that certain events (primarily the Tribulation, or the first half of it) must take place before Christ comes again.

The Millennium

Another related and important question has to do with whether or not the Millennium is literal. Premillenarians believe that Christ will have a literal thousand-year reign: "And I saw thrones, and [the saints] sat upon them, and judgment was given unto them; and I saw the souls of them that were beheaded for the witness of Jesus, and for the Word of God, and which had not worshiped the beast, neither his image, neither had received his mark upon their foreheads or in their hands; and they lived and reigned with Christ a thousand years" (Rev. 20:4). This reign will follow the binding and imprisoning of Satan (20:1-3) so that he may no longer deceive the nations.

Some view the Millennium as an extension and visible expression of Christ's reign in the hearts of His people on earth and in heaven. Others see it as

177

a fulfillment of God's promises to Israel, involving the restoration of the Jews to their homeland as a nation and the reestablishment of a literal throne, king, temple, and sacrificial system.

Many Bible scholars feel that the idea of a literal Millennium cannot be harmonized with biblical eschatology (teaching about the last days). They view the Millennium as a symbol of the ideal Church. Since these people do not believe in an actual millennium, they are called "amillennialists."

Still another amillenarian view says that the symbolic language of The Revelation represents God's working in history, and that the kingdom of God is to be realized through the preaching of the Gospel. The missionary task of the Church, they claim, includes the ultimate Christianizing of society.[53]

Jesus Is Coming!

Whatever points of view expositors take on the Tribulation, the Rapture, and the Millennium, it is thrilling to realize that all agree on the great, glorious, and incontestable fact that *Jesus is coming again*. The details of His next appearance are interesting and important to study, but differences in interpreting these details should never obscure the central *fact* of His coming.

It is significant that neither our Lord nor the prophets and apostles mention the return of Christ for speculative purposes, but always as a motive for practical daily holiness. We could summarize the doctrine: "Since all these things will be destroyed . . . what kind of people should you be? Your lives should be holy and dedicated to God" (2 Peter 3:11, TEV).

Two Resurrections

Some momentous events will take place at the coming of Christ. The resurrection of the believing dead will then occur, and we who are still alive will be glorified (1 Cor. 15:52) and caught up to meet Him in the air (1 Thes. 4:17). The resurrection of the dead is emphasized in the New Testament, but it is taught throughout Scripture. Even Job said, "I know that my Redeemer lives, and at last He will stand upon the earth; and after my skin has thus been destroyed, then out of my flesh I shall see God; whom I myself shall see, whom my own eyes shall behold, and not another" (Job 19:25-27, BERK).

David anticipated this resurrection (Ps. 16:9) and Daniel mentioned it (Dan. 12:1-3). Jesus taught it repeatedly and emphasized that it will include *all* men: "The hour is coming, in the which *all* that are in the graves shall hear His voice, and shall come forth, they that have done good unto the resurrection of life, and they that have done evil unto the resurrection of damnation" (John 5:28, 29).

That the resurrection is a physical rather than a merely spiritual event is proved by the resurrection of Lazarus (John 11:44) and by that of our Lord Himself (Luke 24:39).

The resurrection of the body is part of our total redemption (Rom. 8:23). A Christian should not long to be delivered from the body, with all of its weaknesses and problems, but for the body's redemption. "We sigh deeply while in this tent, not because we want to be stripped of it, but rather to be invested with the other covering, so that the mortal may be absorbed by the real life" (2 Cor. 5:4, BERK). Our resurrection bodies will not be identical with the ones we have now, but will be closely related to them.

Believers will be resurrected at the coming of Christ (1 Thes. 4:16). This will be the *first* resurrection (cf. John 5:28, 29), of which Paul wanted to be part (Phil. 3:11). It is, literally, the resurrection "out of the dead." That is, the righteous will be raised from among the wicked.

There is clearly a time lapse between the resurrection of believers to glory and the resurrection of unbelievers to judgment. Though we cannot be dogmatic as to the *exact* length of this interval, there will be a lapse of at least a thousand years between the two resurrections: "I saw the souls of them that were beheaded for the witness of Jesus, and for the Word of God, and which had not worshiped the beast, neither his image, neither had received his mark upon their foreheads, or in their hands; and they lived and reigned with Christ a thousand years. But the rest of the dead lived not again until the thousand years were finished. . . . Blessed and holy is he that hath part in the first resurrection; on such the second death hath no power, but they shall be priests of God and of Christ and shall reign with Him a thousand years" (Rev. 20:4-6).

The Dead

What about the condition of the dead before they are resurrected? The Scriptures affirm the conscious existence of both the wicked and the righteous after death and before their resurrections, but give few details. It seems clear that the soul is without a body and that believers are in a condition of conscious joy. Unbelievers, however, await the resurrection in a state of suffering (Luke 16: 23). Paul was willing "to be absent from the body and to be present with the Lord" (2 Cor. 5:8). He said referring to death, that he preferred "to depart and be with Christ, which is far better" (Phil. 1:23). Dead believers are at rest: "Blessed are the dead which die in the Lord from henceforth . . . that they may rest from their labors" (Rev. 14:13).

Death is frequently described in the Bible as sleep. In the Old Testament the term "sleep" is applied to *all* the dead, but in the New Testament it applies mostly to the *righteous* dead. Paul used the word only of believers. This term does not apply to the soul or spirit; it does not imply total unconsciousness until the resurrection. It rather implies unconsciousness with reference to *earthly life,* for which consciousness the body is necessary. The dead are "asleep" so far as this world is concerned, but this in no way implies that they are asleep or unconscious to the other world or that their spirits are totally unconscious.

Scripture clearly nowhere teaches "soul sleep." Passages quoted to prove this doctrine refer primarily to bodily, or physical, relations. All that we have said about the state of the righteous dead bears this out.

The consciousness of the unrighteous dead is also clearly taught. They are in prison (1 Peter 3:19), which would be unnecessary if they were unconscious. The story of the rich man and Lazarus (Luke 16:19-31), whatever else it may or may not teach, shows that the unrighteous dead experience conscious suffering and punishment.

No Purgatory

The passages cited clearly refute the doctrine of purgatory. A person dies either as one who has been redeemed or as one who is under judgment. After death there is no passing over from one condition to the other. Final judgment or redemption simply settles what has already begun at the time of death.

More is said about the condition of the dead than about their location. In the Old Testament the souls of all the dead are spoken of as going to sheol, which is translated "grave," "hell," or "pit." "Thou wilt not leave my soul in hell [sheol], neither wilt thou suffer thy holy one to see corruption" (Ps. 16:10). Sheol is a place of sorrow. "The sorrows of hell [sheol] compassed me about" (2 Sam. 22:6), said David. Hades, translated "hell" and "grave," is the New Testament equivalent of sheol. Other New Testament terms for the intermediate state include "paradise" (Luke 12:43) and "Abraham's bosom" (16:22).

The Judgments

But the intermediate state will be succeeded at last by the final judgment, toward which all history is heading. God is the Ruler of all men, the Lawgiver, and the final Judge. Sometimes the Bible mentions God (the Father) as judge: "God the Judge of all" (Heb. 12:23); and sometimes it mentions Christ: "The Lord Jesus Christ . . . shall judge the quick and the dead at His appearing and His kingdom" (2 Tim. 4:1). The relationship of the Father and the Son in judgment is made clear: "He [God the Father] hath appointed a day in the which He will judge the world in righteousness by that Man [Christ] whom He hath ordained, whereof He hath given assurance unto all men, in that He hath raised Him from the dead" (Acts 17:31).

God is judging men and nations continually, but there will be a final judgment which all previous judgments foreshadow. It will be an extension of past and present judgment. An unbeliever *"has been judged* already because he has not believed in the name of the only begotten Son of God" (John 3:18, NAS). A believer, on the other hand, *"has* [present tense] eternal life, and does not come into judgment, but has passed out of death into life" (John 5:24, NAS).

183

The purpose of final judgment will not be to *ascertain* the quality of an individual's character, but to *disclose* his character and to assign him to the eternal place corresponding to what he is because of his trust or lack of trust in God.

Several future judgments are mentioned in Scripture. The judgment of the living nations (Matt. 25:31-46), according to premillennialists, will take place at the return of Christ with His saints. It will lead to the setting up of the millennial kingdom.

Believers will be judged, but not with unbelievers: "We must all appear before the judgment seat of Christ, that every man may receive the things done in his body, according to that he hath done, whether it be good or bad" (2 Cor. 5:10). It is clear that this judgment does not decide a believer's salvation, but appraises his works. A Christian, in this judgment, can suffer loss of reward. "This is a judgment, not for destiny, but for adjustment, for reward or loss, according to our works, for position in the Kingdom: every man according as his work shall be."[54]

The final judgment of the unsaved will be at the great white throne of God. John describes it: "I saw a great white throne and Him that sat on it, from whose face the earth and the heaven fled away; and there was found no place for them. And I saw the dead, small and great, stand before God; and the books were opened; and another book was opened, which is the book of life; and the dead were judged out of those things which were written in the books, according to their works.

And the sea gave up the dead which were in it, and death and hell [hades] delivered up the dead which were in them; and they were judged every man according to their works. And death and hell were cast into the lake of fire. This is the second death. And whosoever was not found written in the book of life was cast into the lake of fire" (Rev. 20:11-15).

The final judgment of Satan will occur just before that of the Great White Throne: "The devil that deceived [men] was cast into the lake of fire and brimstone" (Rev. 20:10). Presumably Satan's angels will be judged at the same time, for Jesus spoke of "everlasting fire prepared for the devil *and his angels*" (Matt. 25:41).

Hell

The final destiny of the wicked is hell. This awesome place is described in various ways. It is a place or state of unquenchable (Mark 9:43) and everlasting (Matt. 25:41) fire. It is spoken of as a lake of fire and brimstone (Rev. 20:10). That figurative language is used in these descriptions may be indicated by the fact that death and hell will be cast into it.

Hell is conceived of as outer darkness (Matt. 8:12). It is described as a place of eternal torment and punishment (Rev. 14:10, 11). If figurative language is involved, it is obviously symbolic of something so awful no one in his right mind could be indifferent to avoiding it. Hell "is the loss of all good, whether physical or spiritual, and the misery of an evil conscience banished from God and the society of the holy and dwelling under God's positive curse forever."[55]

Nowhere in Scripture is there any trace of the idea that hell is a kind of "Jolly Boys' Club," absence from which would cause us to miss our friends. This flippant notion is Satan's lie. Hell is "the blackness of darkness forever" (Jude 13) — utter aloneness. C. S. Lewis once spoke of hell as "nothing but yourself for all eternity"! This is not the whole truth about hell, but it describes one of its most hideous aspects.

The future punishment of the wicked is not annihilation. "In support of the doctrine of conditional immortality [that the lost ultimately cease to exist] it has been urged that other terms descriptive of the fate of the condemned, such as 'perdition,' 'corruption,' 'destruction,' and 'death' point to a cessation of being. This, however, rests on an unscriptural interpretation of these terms, which everywhere in the Old and New Testaments designate a state of existence with an undesirable content — never the pure negation of existence — just as 'life,' in Scripture, describes a positive mode of being, never mere existence as such. Perdition, corruption, destruction, and death [refer to] the welfare of the ethical, spiritual character of man, without implying the annihilation of his physical existence."[56]

There is no biblical evidence for believing in the final restoration of the lost or in the universal salvation of all men. Perhaps the clearest disproof of these notions, as well as of final annihilation, is the fact that *the same word* is used to describe both punishment and life: "These will go away into *eternal* punishment; but the righteous into *eternal* life." However we may try to qualify the word so that it means "age-long" rather than everlasting, we must apply the same qualification to the destinies of the righteous and the wicked. We cannot, consistently, deny eternal punishment without also denying eternal life. And "eternal life" is *everlasting* life. "Eternal" certainly means "everlasting" when it is applied to God. Why should it mean anything else when it modifies "punishment"?

There are, however, *degrees* of punishment in hell and of reward in heaven. Some, at the judgment seat of Christ in heaven, will suffer loss of reward because their works of "wood, hay, and stubble" will not stand the test of fire (1 Cor. 3:15). Their capacity for enjoyment, though unlimited in duration, will be less than that of others. Similarly, the wicked will be judged, "every man according to his works" (Rev. 20:13). "That servant who knew his Lord's will and prepared not himself, neither did according to His will, shall be beaten with many stripes; but he that knew not, and did commit things worthy of stripes, shall be beaten with few stripes" (Luke 12:47, 48).

God, in His love, has done everything necessary to deliver men from eternal punishment. His justice requires that He punish sin, but His love provides salvation freely for all who will accept it. Those in hell are there because they refused or ignored God's love; they are solely responsible for their condition. The realization of this truth will surely be one of the most painful experiences of perdition.

Heaven

The final destiny of the righteous is heaven. Heaven is most simply defined as where God is. It is a place of rest (Heb. 4:9), of glory (2 Cor. 4:17), of holiness (Rev. 21:27), of worship (Rev. 19:1), of fellowship with others (Heb. 12:23), and of being with God (Rev. 21:3). He "shall wipe away all tears from their eyes; and there shall be no more death, neither sorrow, nor crying, neither shall there be any more pain; for the former things are passed away" (Rev. 21:4).

Believers may receive one or more crowns — the crown of life (James 1:12), the crown of glory (1 Peter 5:4), and the crown of righteousness (2 Tim. 4:8). Those who have been won for Christ through our witness become our crown of rejoicing (1 Thes. 2:19).

Everything in heaven will be new: "The earth also, and the works that are therein, shall be burned up. . . . Nevertheless we, according to His promise, look for new heavens and a new earth, wherein dwelleth righteousness" (2 Peter 3:10, 13). John reports that he "saw a new heaven and a new earth; for the first heaven and the first earth were passed away, and there was no more sea And I . . . saw the holy city, new Jerusalem, coming down from God out of heaven. . . . And they shall reign forever and ever" (Rev. 21:1, 2; 22:5).

God's kingdom will be established when all things

are put under His feet. Then, "at the name of Jesus, every knee shall bow and every tongue confess that Jesus Christ is Lord, to the glory of God the Father" (Phil. 2:10, 11). The kingdoms of this world shall be the kingdoms of our Lord, and He shall reign forever and ever. His will will be done on earth as it is done in heaven.

Heaven will not be the boring experience of strumming a harp on a cloud, as some facetiously characterize it. It will be the most dynamic, expanding, exhilarating experience conceivable. Our problem now is that, with our finite minds, we cannot imagine it.

> When we've been there ten thousand years,
>   Bright shining as the Sun,
> We've no less days to sing His praise,
>   Than when we first begun.

For Further Reading

Hamilton, Floyd. *The Basis of Millennial Faith.* Grand Rapids: Eerdmans, 1942.

Ladd, George E. *Crucial Questions About the Kingdom of God.* Grand Rapids: Eerdmans, 1952.

Pentecost, J. Dwight. *Things to Come.* Findlay, Ohio: Dunham Pub. Co., 1958.

Reese, Alexander. *The Approaching Advent of Christ.* London: Marshall, Morgan, & Scott, (n.d.)

Vos, Geerhardus. *The Pauline Eschatology.* Grand Rapids: Eerdmans, 1952.

Notes

Chapter 1

[1]B. B. Warfield, *The Inspiration and Authority of the Bible* (New York: Oxford University Press, 1927), p. 299.
[2]T. C. Hammond, *In Understanding Be Men* (Chicago: Inter-Varsity Press, 1968), p. 13.
[3]J. N. Birdsell, "Canon of the New Testament," in *New Bible Dictionary* (*NBD*) (Grand Rapids: Eerdmans, 1962), p. 194.
[4]W. F. Albright, *Archaeology and the Religion of Israel* (Baltimore: Johns Hopkins Press, 1942), p. 176.
[5]Nelson Glueck, *Rivers in the Desert* (New York: Farrar, Straus, & Giroux, 1959), p. 31.

Chapter 2

[6]A. H. Strong, *Systematic Theology* (Philadelphia: Judson Press, 1907), p. 255.
[7]Hammond, *In Understanding*, p. 44.
[8]R. A. Finlayson, "Holiness," *NBD*, p. 530.
[9]*Ibid.*, p 530.
[10]R. A. Finlayson, "Trinity," *NBD*, p. 1298.
[11]*Ibid.*, p. 1298.
[12]*Ibid.*, p. 1300.
[13]Hammond, *In Understanding*, p. 54.
[14]Finlayson, "Trinity," *NBD*, p. 1300.